Daily Spiritual Nugget

Spiritual Nuggets: Prayers for Your Daily Walk

Daily Spiritual Nugget

Spiritual Nuggets: Prayers for Your Daily Walk

Copyright © 2014 by Deacon Shawn W. Ashworth, Ed.D

ISBN: 978-1502711243

All rights reserved. No part of this book may be reproduced or transmitted in any form or by any means, electronic or mechanical, including photocopying, recording, or by any information storage or retrieval system, without permission in writing from the copyright owner.

Scripture references are from the following sources: The Holy Bible, New International Version (NIV). Copyright © 1973,1978,1984 by Biblica, Inc. Used by permission of Zonderdan. All rights reserved worldwide.

Editor: Athena Hernandez

Cover Design: Dwayne Herbert

To order additional copies of this book, contact:

spiritualnugget@gmail.com

Foreward

Having watched this author over the past few years after coming to our community, it is evident that she is on a mission for growth, both spiritually and emotionally. Her commitment to her beliefs and standards are exciting and the experiences of her life have developed her in a very positive way.

"ASK and you shall receive, SEEK and you shall find, KNOCK and the door shall be opened" (Matthew 7:7).

Dr. Shawn Ashworth has taken what life has to offer, both the negative and positive, and has advanced to the next levels in her life.

As you read this book thoughtfully and prayerfully, it will strengthen you to never give up! It is my most profound pleasure to witness the awesomeness of Dr. Ashworth. Every chapter, line and verse is the life experiences of the writer but also speaks to the sentiment of the reader.

Thank you, Dr. Ashworth, for trusting me to pen these few words.

Bishop Wilbert L. Baltimore, DD, PhD
Kings Apostle Church World Ministries
Holy Temple Cathedral Church

Dedication

It was God who blessed me with this gift of ministering to His people through my Daily Nuggets, and so I humbly dedicate this blessing to Him, who has given me an abundance of courage and strength to tell my story of how God made me whole.

I am very grateful for friends and family who have encouraged me to keep sharing God's word, and I thank everyone who has confirmed my gift from God, by letting me know how the Nuggets were blessing them.

To God's servants who obediently preached the Word of God on Sunday's, which stirred my spirit; teaching me how to believe, trust, and fall in love with a man who would love me unconditionally, in spite of my faults. Thank you Pastor Jamesetta Davis and Apostle Wilbert L. Baltimore, for allowing God to use you to guide me along my spiritual walk.

Brandon and Taylor, I love you both very much. You are the reason why I have stayed steadfast on this spiritual journey so that you both can reap the many blessings that God has stored up for you and your families. My "life lesson" talks were all orchestrated by Him, who loves you too! Thank you for your support and allowing me to share your space with so many others because of my passion for serving others.

TABLE OF CONTENTS

God is Love 1

Faith, Hope, and Joy 13

Wisdom Thinking 23

Creating a Pure Heart 34

His Word and His Way 43

Total Praise 54

Perfect Peace 66

Grateful 75

Grace and Mercy 84

Constant Companion 95

Strength 105

Protection 115

Reflection and Practice 125

Additional Prayers for Healing 128

Daily Spiritual Nugget

Daily Spiritual Nugget

God Is Love

Tina Turner won critical acclaim for her song, *"What's Love Got to Do With It"* many years ago. The song resonated with women and men, describing the hurt and lack of love they felt in relationships, marriages, and even with family. During the course of my marriage, I would often recite the lyrics of this once-famous song after instances when my ex-husband demeaned my character and sabotaged my spirit with physical and verbal abuse. Each time, he would conclude with "I love you." My thoughts always retreated to the same two questions: What kind of love was I dealing with, and why was I accepting this type of love? I knew God, and I knew He loved me, and that love did not hurt! Ephesians 5:25 tells husbands to love their wives just as Christ loved the church….I was definitely not feeling that kind of love. God's Word also told me that love was patient, kind, and joyful, not disrespectful, intimidating, and demeaning.

It took me a minute, but I finally realized that God's love was all I needed! God, all by himself, was love; it was the love that I was looking for, and definitely the love I needed. I thank God daily for reminding me who He is, and that He loves unconditionally in spite of myself. His love protects me from harm and danger, and from those who mistreat me. God's love is the only love that forgives, and loves even more. God's love never fails, it never gives up, it never demeans, and it never runs out on us.

    I learned that through the good and the bad, and in sickness and health, God will never leave us alone. He actually wraps his arms tighter around us, comforting us and providing assurance that He has us right where we are supposed to be. Praising God is what we should do! He will not take us through anything He hasn't prepared us to handle. In the midst of providing us the love we are seeking, He shows us how to love again; unconditionally and with wisdom.

    God's love allowed me to trust again, and to believe again. His love taught me to be cautious and careful about the company I kept, and those that I allowed in my personal space. Through His love, I learned not to settle, but instead to always seek out the best in myself, and most definitely, the best in others. He gave me a voice that began to speak up about my wants and desires, and not to settle for what was left behind. He filled my heart with good thoughts, and showed me how to quickly rebuke the thoughts and emotions that would cause me to cry, be nervous, or fearful. The Lord stole my heart—And I loved the feeling that consumed my mind, body, and soul. He became my "soul" provider of love, peace, and joy. I am so grateful that I chose to fall in love with my Lord and Savior.

Do you know love? How do you define love? What kind of love are you experiencing?

How do you define love?

"The Lord appeared to us in the past, saying: "I have loved you with an everlasting love; I have drawn you with unfailing kindness."

Lord, I am so glad that I can count on you, especially when others hurt or disappoint me. Thank you Lord, for loving me unconditionally in spite of myself. For being in my presence showing me how to love, be loved, and how to accept love. I will reciprocate your kindness by praising and honoring your precious name. Hallelujah!
Jeremiah 31:3 NIV

~~~~~

"If I have the gift of prophecy and can fathom all mysteries and all knowledge, and if I have a faith that can move mountains, but do not have love, I am nothing."

Lord, Your Word says that love is patient, kind, and love always protects and persevere. Thank you God for reminding me that my deeds and my works mean nothing unless they are done in love. Lord I pray that my daily actions and reactions exemplify the same love that You show me, especially when I have been offended, hurt, and mistreated by others. Thank you for teaching me how to love myself first, and then others....even my enemies. Through You Lord, I have learned to love unconditionally. Thank you!
1 Corinthians 13:2 NIV

Daily Spiritual Nugget

"It always protects, always trusts, always hopes, always perseveres."

Lord, thank you for loving me in spite of myself. Your love has also taught me to love in spite of the evil ways of others. Thank you for Your unconditional love; it has taught me to love the same way in spite of…..

1 Corinthians 13:7 NIV

"Give thanks to the Lord for he is good; his love endures forever."

Just remember that God will always be your greatest fan; He will love you no matter what. In spite of any good or bad, He will always be committed to you for the rest of your life. Even when you don't feel the love of others, know that His love is always present.

Psalm 107:1 NIV

"Whoever does not love does not know God, because God is love."

God, thank you for modeling how to love unconditionally, especially towards those who show no love and are only lovers of themselves. Love does not hate or seek evil. Your Word says that love is patient and kind. Thank you for being my love, peace, joy, friend, and protector during my storms in this life.

1 John 4:8 NIV

"He himself bore our sins" in his body on the cross, so that we might die to sins and live for righteousness; "by his wounds you have been healed."
Thank you Jesus! This daily walk is hard, but I am at peace knowing that my mistakes and sometimes ignorant moments are already forgiven. I am in awe of your love for me in spite of my wrong doing. I am full of joy because I know your spirit resides in me, and it keeps me from evil. Thank you for all of your protection!
1 Peter 2:24 NIV

"The grass withers and the flowers fall, but the word of our God endures forever."
Through the good and the bad, God will always be around to provide comfort and peace to your mind, body, and soul. He is your constant companion.
Isaiah 40:8 NIV

**"Give thanks to the Lord, for he is good;
his love endures forever."**
Lord, thank you for your everlasting commitment to love me. You are my one and true love; faithful, always present, and always forgiving.
1 Chronicles 16:34 NIV

"But seek first his kingdom and his righteousness, and all these things will be given to you as well."
Thank you God for providing me the energy to seek after your ways and precepts. I want to be just like you. Remind me daily of those things that make you happy!
Matthew 6:33 NIV

"Have I not commanded you? Be strong and courageous. Do not be afraid; do not be discouraged, for the Lord your God will be with you wherever you go."

Thank you Lord for having my back. For being there when others are not. For showing me how to handle those things that cause fear and anxiety and allowing me to still be victorious! Amen

Joshua 1:9 NIV

~~~~~

"He says, "Be still, and know that I am God; I will be exalted among the nations, I will be exalted in the earth."

Thank you God for taking care of my heart's desire. For showing me who you are by the awesome wonders and blessings you have allowed me to reap.

Psalm 46:10 NIV

~~~~~

"Take delight in the lord, and he will give you the desires of your heart."

Thank you God for honoring me with your love because I have honored you with my time, talents and commitment. I know that when I lean on you and trust in you to take care of all my concerns you bless me with things I don't even ask for. Thank you!

Psalm 37:4 NIV

"The sting of death is sin, and the power of sin is the law. But thanks be to God! He gives us the victory through our Lord Jesus Christ."
Thank You Lord for the victory! Your death on the cross has set me free. I am so grateful for Your Word, it is full of examples of how much You love me. Thank You Lord for Your grace and mercy. I thank You for always guiding me; delivering me from harm's way and causing the evil to flee from me. Thank You for restoring my faith; I am trusting in Your promise to bless me abundantly.
1 Corinthians 15:56-57 NIV

"Blessed is the one you discipline, Lord , the one you teach from your law; you grant them relief from days of trouble, till a pit is dug for the wicked."
Thank You Lord for the teaching of Your Word. It provides me with instructions on who to fellowship with, what to eat and wear, and how to seek You so that I live free from the bondage of sin; reaping a continuous flow of blessings. Your Word says that You chastise those You love, so Lord I don't mind Your correction. I know I may question Your motives at times for some of the challenges I face in my life, but I realize that You are just checking to see how much I depend on and how much I really trust You. I am careful to not take any credit for what I say I do, but to give You glory for all that You do! Thank You Lord God for Your Word that protects me from the evil ways of others, gives me joy when I am sad, and tells me how much You love me unconditionally.
Psalm 94:12-13 NIV

"Love the Lord your God with all your heart and with all your soul and with all your strength."
Lord God I love You, honor You, and will worship You forever with everything I am, and all that I have. My strength is because of You, and all that You promise to do. My heart is wide open to give and to receive. Because of You I can breathe. Thank You for my existence. Because of You I have peace, thank You for helping me to think clearly. Because of You I have courage, I can walk with my head up high and not in shame. It is because of You that I rejoice when others try to steal my joy.
Deuteronomy 6:5 NIV

"The Lord appeared to us in the past, saying: "I have loved you with an everlasting love; I have drawn you with unfailing kindness."
Lord I am so glad that I can count on you, especially when others hurt or disappoint me. Thank you Lord for loving me unconditionally in spite of myself. For being in my presence showing me how to love, be loved and how to accept love. I will reciprocate your kindness by praising and honoring your precious name. Hallelujah!
Jeremiah 31:3 NIV

"He who did not spare his own Son, but gave him up for us all--how will he not also, along with him, graciously give us all things?"

Thank you God for the ultimate sacrifice! Just for me, in spite of all my stuff, you continue to provide everything I need. The blessings are always on time indeed! The desires of my heart are comforted by your eternal love, and my mind rests in peace knowing how much you care. When others are not, you are always there!

Romans 8:32 NIV

"Love does not delight in evil but rejoices with the truth. It always protects, always trusts, always hopes, always perseveres."

Lord thank you for your unconditional love. You always seem to provide me with just what I need. Continue to show me how to show that same kind of love towards others; especially towards my enemies, and those who mistreat me directly or indirectly. I pray for hope and peace in love.

1Corinthians 13:6-7 NIV

"But love your enemies, do good to them, and lend to them without expecting to get anything back. Then your reward will be great, and you will be children of the Most High, because he is kind to the ungrateful and wicked."

Wow Lord! Love in spite of..... I want to walk in Your favor Lord. I want to make sure that my life is aligned with Your Will and Your Way. So I pray for continuous strength to forgive my enemies of the pain they have caused. Continue to show me how to keep my heart pure and filled with love for them. I pray that my actions and reactions are delivered in peace and that my words are pleasing to Your ears.

Luke 6:35 NIV

~~~~~

"Because of the lord's great love we are not consumed, for his compassions never fail. They are new every morning; great is your faithfulness."

Thank you Lord for loving me enough to keep me out of harm's way. I am so grateful for Your mercy each and every day. Thank you for having my back when I pray.

Lamentations 3:22-23 NIV

Faith, Hope, Joy

Faith is knowing that what we hope for, even if we can't see it, is attainable. I had such little faith in the late 1990s. At times life felt hopeless, but I hoped for everything. For my house to become a home, for me to be safe, for mental strength, and most of all, I hoped for peace from my marital storms. I only experienced and knew what joy looked like outside of my home. When I realized that my children were suffering, I gave my heart, mind, and soul to God, and pleaded for Him to take control. God's Word and His Way saved *my* life—saved *our* lives. I learned to rest in his arms, and allowed Him to take control. When I would begin to lose faith, the Holy Spirit attacked my pain and suffering, and reminded me that enough was enough. God's voice whispered: "I got you, just keep giving it to me." God kept showing me Psalm 30:5—"weeping may stay for a night, but joy comes in the morning." Oh, and it did—another one of God's promises kept! I no longer allow my faith to waiver.

I hope in the Lord, and not in people. I don't allow others to steal my joy, because they lack some of their own. I learned to not give my circumstances any attention, but instead to give them a faithful glance and let God have His way. I chose to put my faith in God, and not in man. I chose to live a life of peace, joy, and pure happiness. I chose not to fear man, but fear God with a spirit of hope for salvation. Jesus became the center of my heart, my joy, and the whole of my existence. He became the music in my ears, always providing a sweet melody of his love, peace, and forgiveness.

    The key to knowing the extent of God's faith in you is to stay in a relationship with Him. I submerged myself into his Word, His music, and His angels he sent to stand around me. I began to commune with Him daily in prayer and worship. He opened my heart to see, hear, and feel joy on a more regular basis. This allowed me to see and receive all of His blessings; He was just waiting for me to have faith in Him.

    I came to realize that faith in God provided a type of joy that could not be explained. My joy was strong, it was peaceful, and it felt good to know that because of it, I did not have to struggle with hopelessness. When I call on Him, he always provides just what I need, not what I want. How strong is your faith? What are you hoping in, and are you sure it will bring you the joy of the Lord?

Faith, Hope and Joy, do you have them, and how do you get them?

"But someone will say, "You have faith: I have deeds." Show me your faith without deeds, and I will show you my faith by my deeds."
Lord, help me not to judge. Give me courage to step out on faith, to hear you, and to keep me from doing things in an unfaithful way. Lord, give me the strength to do things that I doubt and the faith that you're there to step in when I'm weak. Grant me peace, knowing that I am to put all that I know and do into you, and that you will take care of me as long as I believe in You.
James 2:18 NIV

"Shout for joy to the Lord all the earth".
I am thankful and rejoice for my family, peace, finances, joy, health, trials, tribulations, pain, and work. I acknowledge you in all things, and I am comforted in your presence.
Psalm 100:1 NIV

"And if we know that he hears us—whatever we ask—we know that we have what we asked of him."
Lord, thank you for listening to my requests. I know they are a lot. Lord, I believe in my heart that You are my "soul" provider. Help and keep me focused on my commitment to depend on You. Lord, I thank you for considering my requests. Lord, I ask for favor for friends, family, and my enemies. Help them believe in You and then in themselves. Create in them pure hearts and a desire to live right. Give them confidence. Give them healthy bodies, give them direction.
1 John 5:15 NIV

"Do not be like them, for your Father knows what you need before you ask him."

Lord, I am solely depending on You to find me a perfect mate. Someone who knows and loves You. Someone who finds joy in talking about You and studying Your Word. He has to love me just like You love Your people. He has to love You more. He has to be a man who is a provider that also takes the time to spend with You, and then me.

Matthew 6:8 NIV

"The Son is the image of the invisible God, the firstborn over all creation. For in him all things were created: things in heaven and on earth, visible and invisible, whether thrones or powers or rulers or authorities; all things have been created through him and for him."

Lord, thank you for being in charge of everything around me, in me, and for me! My faith in your works will always be in my heart so that I am sure to give you praise for your constant protection. Thank you for keeping me safe from my enemies.

Colossians 1:15-16 NIV

"You will keep in perfect peace those whose minds are steadfast, because they trust in you."

Lord, you have taught me and shown me over and over the value of possessing a faithful spirit. I have vowed to remain faithful to your way. I am so thankful to you for showing me how to find peace in my mind, for my body, and in my spirit. Thank you for giving me perfect peace in the midst of my storms.

Isaiah 26:3 NIV

"How beautiful on the mountains are the feet of those who bring good news, who proclaim peace, who bring good tidings, who proclaim salvation, who say to Zion, "Your God reigns!""

I put all my trust into you, Lord. Thank you for being large and in charge over my health, finances, and relationships! Your Word directs my path. My faith keeps me at peace on the journey towards salvation.

Isaiah 52:7 NIV

~~~~~

"Now faith is confidence in what we hope for and assurance about what we do not see."

Lord, I am so glad that the Holy Spirit reminds me of your love and promise to care for me. Sometimes I struggle in the faith walk; where doubt sets in and I am unsure about what to do with life's problems. I know there is power in the tongue, and so God help me to speak life into my body, mind, sickness, health, relationships, family, in school, and on my job. Thank you for giving me hope in your Word. Hallelujah!

Hebrews 11:1 NIV

~~~~~

"Make every effort to live in peace with everyone and to be holy; without holiness no one will see the Lord."

Lord, I thank you for showing me the power of prayer. For you have taught me that prayer provides the peace that keeps me confident in my daily walk, when others try to destroy my spirit. I thank you for living in me, so that I treat those same people with love, creating peaceful relationships.

Hebrews 12:14 NIV

"May the God of hope fill you with all joy and peace as you trust in him, so that you may overflow with hope by the power of the Holy Spirit."
Lord I rejoice in recognizing the impact that Your presence has had in my life. I am not the same person I was! I thank You for the Holy Spirit, who has stepped in to keep me from causing pain and acting evil, & from allowing others to do the same to me. Daily, I renew my faith and pray for Your power, strength and hope to reside in me.
Romans 15:13 NIV

"For the word of God is alive and active. Sharper than any double-edged sword, it penetrates even to dividing soul and spirit, joints and marrow; it judges the thoughts and attitudes of the heart."
Thank you Lord for your Word, and for keeping me grounded in what I say and do. Thank you for keeping my spirit alive and full of peace, joy, thanksgiving, and love.
Hebrews 4:12 NIV

**"Because of the lord's great love we are not consumed, for his compassions never fail.
They are new every morning; great is your faithfulness."**
Thank you Lord for Your steadfast attention towards me; for keeping me protected from harm; and delivering me from sickness, selfishness, and sin. For every day that You give me an opportunity to start over; turning my wrongs into rights; and the strength to fight through the tribulations in my life; Lord, I thank You! Thank you for Your love, joy, and peace, and for caring about me! Hallelujah!
Lamentations 3:22 NIV

Daily Spiritual Nugget

"Blessed are the poor in spirit, for theirs is the kingdom of heaven."
Lord, thank You for Your Word which provides the blue print for my walk on this earth. I pray that everything I do, speak, and think is pleasing to you. I am always careful to seek Your voice and spirit first, to help provide me with wisdom to handle my fears, life's challenges, and those trials and tribulations that I experience with others. I have total faith in You!
Matthew 5:3 NIV

"Be joyful in hope, patient in affliction, faithful in prayer."
Thank you God for teaching and showing me the blessings of being faithful in Your Word by praying and fasting, and waiting patiently for You to reveal Your glory. Having faith is having hope in the Holy Spirit's power to take away the worries of this life, and restoring my heart with joy, providing comfort to my soul.
Romans 12:12 NIV

"Who is wise and understanding among you? Let them show it by their good life, by deeds done in the humility that comes from wisdom."
Lord, I pray daily that my words and actions towards others are pleasing in your sight and represent you! I am thankful for your wise words and I give you glory for who I am, and your plans for who I am to be!
James 3:13 NIV

"In addition to all this, take up the shield of faith, with which you can extinguish all the flaming arrows of the evil one".
Lord thank you for Your mighty hand of power that provides a way out of no way.
I thank you for the strong covering which protects me from myself, others and evil things of this world. Thank you for providing clarity in my mind so that I have a steadfast focus on just what I need to do when chaos & evil come my way; experiencing a sound mind of peace in the midst of the storms! Hallelujah!
Ephesians 6:16 NIV

~~~~~

"I lift up my eyes to the mountains— where does my help come from? My help comes from the Lord, the Maker of heaven and earth."
Lord I am so glad that where ever I am, all I need to do is raise my hands and look up to speak to You, and You are there! The maker of all things good; I put my trust in You always..... Not man, not substance nor idols. You are my light, which gives me peace in the midst of my storms. You are my comforter when I feel alone. You are my joy that keeps my heart pure; not committing evil and causing others pain. You are the sweet taste in my mouth that keeps me from speaking evil and telling lies. You are my everything and everything is right!
Psalm 121:1-2 NIV

"Humble yourselves, therefore, under God's mighty hand, that he may lift you up in due time."
God I will always be mindful to give you the glory for everything good that comes down my dwelling. Even on my worst days, I know you are just trying to get my attention because there is something you want me to learn. I am not ashamed to tell others that I am love because of You; I am hopeful because of You; I am at peace because of You. I live because of You!
1Peter 5:6 NIV

"Be joyful in hope, patient in affliction, faithful in prayer."
Lord thank you for giving me strength while dealing with the chaos in my life. I will not complain as I go through, but instead will pray for peace in my heart, and joy in my spirit during the midst of these storms. Your Word says joy comes in the morning, and so Lord I will wait on You to deliver the blessings that are stored up for me to receive. I have hope, and stand in expectation that You will do just what You say You are going to do! Hallelujah!!
Romans 12:12 NIV

"Now the Lord is the Spirit, and where the Spirit of the Lord is, there is freedom."
Thank you Lord for allowing your Spirit to dwell in me. As it dwells, I rebuke those things that tend to keep chaos, confusion, and adversity around. I pray that freedom from them occurs daily, and that my spirit reflects peace, joy, and love towards those I encounter. Amen!
2 Corinthians 3:17 NIV

Wisdom Thinking

I am not sure if my thinking was always wise; there were plenty of decisions that I made that I often question myself now. I did finally realize after spending time in God's Word, that He gives us our minds to think of those things wise and good. Our thoughts are to be used to glorify Him. Our job is to think and then pray, and ask God to send the Holy Spirit to guide our every thought, action, and reaction.

Wisdom thinking isn't just about how we think, or what we think about. I have realized that wisdom thinking begins in the heart--what you feel and what you do with those feelings. When we are confronted by trauma, chaos, abuse, loss of loved ones, the heart feels pain. We all know that being in pain is not a happy time.

A quote we're all familiar with begins with "Your thoughts become your actions……" This quote speaks to wisdom thinking. The message appropriately suggests a thought that everything we do is connected to something else that ultimately impacts our journey in life. Every choice brings about a consequence; we just need to be ready to suffer, or be blessed, as a result of our decisions. I realize that wisdom does not always come naturally. It is something that we should ask and pray God to bless us with in all circumstances.

 Using God's Word as a foundation for how I maneuvered through life was my answer. His Word saved my soul, my spirit, and my mind. During one of the roughest times in my life, God's Word became my voice. I intentionally spent the time with Him so that when I spoke, it was His words that spoke out of my heart, and I would be sure to align my thoughts so that my actions would be pleasing in God's sight.

 I pray that my walk is His walk. That He continues to open my eyes and my ears to see and hear the things that He would have me to know. I am allowing Him to guide me in a way that allows me to grow in Him. My mind is now consumed with good thoughts that speak to my heart, so that I may always remember to praise Him in spite of...

 When we think by the spirit, we live a life filled with an abundance of blessings. Stand still and let God go to work. Let His thinking become your thinking. Are you seeking wisdom so that your walk on this earth pleases God?

How do you seek wisdom?

"Be strong and very courageous. Be careful to obey all the law my servant Moses gave you: do not turn from it to the right or to the left, that you may be successful wherever you go."
Lord help me to be strong in Your Word so that my actions are full of courageous behaviors. Provide me with confidence to do a good work in my home, among my peers, and on my job, so that others will see the gifts from you that have helped afford me with other opportunities.
Joshua 1:7 NIV

~~~~~

"But the wisdom that comes from heaven is first of all pure; then peace-loving, considerate, submissive, full of mercy and good fruit, impartial and sincere. Peacemakers who sow in peace reap a harvest of righteousness."
Thank you Holy Spirit for your presence when I am being tested by worldly ways and my heart and mind want to speak and do evil. Lord I thank you for the wisdom that shows me how to act and treat others, even toward those who do not reciprocate those qualities back. Thank you for the peace that rests in my soul, when crisis and chaos arise!
To God be all the glory!
James 3:17-18 NIV

"The tongue has the power of life and death, and those who love it will eat its fruit."
Lord, let the words of my mouth be the meditation of my heart and always be acceptable in your sight. God help me to use my words for good and not for evil. That even when I don't like or agree with what others are saying, you will remind me to speak in a manner that is loving and comforting; always speaking in truth and out of love.
Proverbs 18:21 NIV

~~~~~

"For the Spirit God gave us does not make us timid, but gives us power, love and self-discipline."
Thank you God for allowing your spirit to dwell within me, which makes me feel courageous among my enemies. In moments of weakness, I am strong. I am grateful for the wisdom that helps provide peace when chaos arises.
2 Timothy 1:7 NIV

~~~~~

"Commit to the Lord whatever you do, and he will establish your plans."
When you put God in charge of everything you do and speak of, He provides a way out of no way. Thank you God for reminding me to put you in charge.
Proverbs 16:3 NIV

"Be wise in the way you act toward outsiders; make the most of every opportunity. Let your conversation be always full of grace, seasoned with salt, so that you may know how to answer everyone."
Lord, thank you in advance for choosing my words so that they provoke encouragement and not evil. Thank you for transparency so that my words speak truth and not lies. That even in the midst of my anger and hurt, that I would still speak words of endearment.
Colossians 4:5-6 NIV

"Trust in the Lord forever, for the Lord, the Lord himself, is the Rock eternal."
Lord you are my rock, my redeemer, and my deliverer! Keep me from inflicting self-doubt and allowing others to create confusion in my thinking. I will trust in your ways all the days of my life because your way is the only way.
Isaiah 26:4 NIV

"Do nothing out of selfish ambition or vain conceit. Rather, in humility value others above yourselves, not looking to your own interests but each of you to the interests of the others."
Thank you God for blessing me with the spirit of giving. For showing me how to suspend self-interest in order to help others.
Philippians 2:3-4 NIV

"Jesus replied: 'Love the Lord your God with all your heart and with all your soul and with all your mind.' This is the first and greatest commandment. And the second is like it: 'Love your neighbor as yourself'."
Lord, there is no greater love then the love that I have for You. Your Word teaches me that I will earn an inheritance beyond my thoughts, if I just seek You first! I know I can depend on You to hear, see, and act without judgment, unlike man sometimes seems to do. I pray that my internal light is more than enough to share with others; and because I am blessed, that they are also blessed.
Matthew 22:37-39 NIV

~~~~~

"Whoever loves discipline loves knowledge, but whoever hates correction is stupid."
Thank you God for using Your Word to teach me how to love, treat others, and live righteous. Even during those times when I didn't quite understand, You showed me through my chaotic moments the way I should go! Thank you for taking control of my thoughts and actions. I am forever grateful! Lord, thank you for showing me how to handle corrective criticism and using my mistakes to make wiser decisions.
Proverbs 12:1 NIV

"But God chose the foolish things of the world to shame the wise; God chose the weak things of the world to shame the strong."
God, thank you for showing me those little things that have gotten me caught up; causing me to lose my focus on you. I know that all that I have is because of you. Thank you for the many blessings, and the opportunities to try and get it right. It is because of your son Jesus that I have wisdom, that I am acceptable in your sight, and that I have chosen to live according to your Word. I am nothing without You and everything with You, Lord.
1 Corinthians 1:27 NIV

~~~~~

"Keep on loving one another as brothers and sisters. Do not forget to show hospitality to strangers, for by so doing some people have shown hospitality to angels without knowing it."
You never know who God has put in your path to bless you, help you, and to keep you out of harm's way. Treat others just like you would want to be treated at all times. Speak and show respect even if they are perfect strangers. Don't make the mistake of pushing your angels away!
Hebrews 13:1 NIV

"For he is the kind of person who is always thinking about the cost. Eat and drink, he says to you, but his heart is not with you."
Lord, let my inner man align with my outer man. For it is my inner man that tells the story. Give me the internal navigator that navigates on the outside with praise and thanksgiving. Let my words and actions bless those who see me just in appearance before words are uttered. True alignment is what I am striving for, in Your name.
Proverbs 23:7 NIV

"But the wisdom that comes from heaven is first of all pure; then peace-loving, considerate, submissive, full of mercy and good fruit, impartial and sincere. Peacemakers who sow in peace reap a harvest of righteousness."
Thank you Holy Spirit for your presence when I am being tested by worldly ways and my heart and mind want to speak and do evil. Lord I thank you for the wisdom that shows me how to act and treat others. Even to those who do not reciprocate those qualities back. Thank you for the peace that rests in my soul, when crisis and chaos arise! To God be all the glory!
James 3:17-18 NIV

"For I command you today to love the Lord your God, to walk in obedience to him, and to keep his commands, decrees and laws; then you will live and increase, and the Lord your God will bless you in the land you are entering to possess."

God has promised to provide you with all your needs and desires. His only request is that you live according to His Word. When you do this, many blessings come--especially those that are unexpected.

Deuteronomy 30:16 NIV

~~~~~

"Jesus looked at them and said, "With man this is impossible, but with God all things are possible."

Thank you Lord for making all things possible. I am forever indebted to you. You always make a way for me to see clearly through my storms. Even if it takes me time to see and hear you. You provide the answers. I rely on your guidance and wisdom to make all things new. Thank you for taking my pain away. Because of you, I am stronger, wiser, and confident that no weapon formed against me shall prosper!

Matthew 19:26 NIV

"Do not be wise in your own eyes; fear the Lord and shun evil. This will bring health to your body and nourishment to your bones."

Thank you God for imparting your wisdom in me; so that I am not left to my own understanding. Your wise and wonderful ways keeps me from doing evil. I pray that my words and my ways are pleasing in your sight. I delight in your love, and thank you for being my Prince of Peace and my Divine Healer. I trust you Lord. Have your way with my mind and body for your glory!

Proverbs 3:7 NIV

~~~~~

"And he who searches our hearts knows the mind of the Spirit, because the Spirit intercedes for God's people in accordance with the will of God."

Thank You God! I pray daily for Your presence in and around me. Thank You in advance for interceding during those moments when I can't find the right words to speak; when my thoughts are in a state of confusion and when others try to test my emotions and patience! Lord God, I thank You for knowing just when to step in and show Your power. I pray that you continue to search my heart, and reveal any imperfections that are not aligned to Your Will and Your Way.

Romans 8:27 NIV

Creating a Pure Heart

Psalm 51, my favorite scripture, reminds me not to become like my chaos. It's helped me learn forgiveness, to treat my enemy with love and in peace, in spite of how I was treated. When you are hurt by others, or offended and mistreated by someone, your first thought is to retaliate; your initial thoughts may wish all kinds of evil things to come their way! That was me. My excuse was that I was human, and God understood. What I came to realize was that I was hurting myself, destroying my heart, and preventing others from seeing the good in me and the God in me.

I was being manipulated, and kept in bondage from living the way I wanted to live; and I didn't even know it! I was told that I was the bad one; that nobody would want me; that I was stupid along with a laundry list of other demeaning characteristics. And then God took control. I began reciting a verse of scripture: *"Cleanse me with hyssop, and I will be clean; wash me, and I will be whiter than snow."* I prayed that God would make my heart pure and clean from 'stinking thinking,' and that He would *"Create in me a pure heart, O God, and renew a steadfast spirit within me."* My prayer was for a renewed sweet spirit within me, so that I could learn how to love again. I believed God to create in me a sound mind that I could make wiser decisions about my circumstance.

    I found out that transparency is the key to a pure heart, mind, body and soul; and I had to confess to God my evil thoughts and ways. I heard the chains falling, my heart was finally loosed, and God was creating a pure heart within me! I learned to live by a code that spoke of peace, envisioned joy, and focused on loving all people, even those who mistreated me. I am so glad that God penetrated my heart during the lowest point in my life; He filled it with forgiveness and freedom from hatred and scorn. I remembered my pain, but my new heart reacted differently. It transformed into a vessel pumping with forgiveness and understanding. I massaged it with good thoughts and kept it warm by wrapping it daily with God's word. I began walking around with a heart that could feel, taste, and see a life full of purpose for me. I was somebody!

    My heart acquired a voice. I used it to formulate words that were full of sweetness, even when positive words were not reciprocated. My heart became a place of comfort, and I asked God to fill it with good thoughts. What kind of heart do you have? How do you handle when others try to crush your heart?

How do you guard your heart?

"Have mercy on me, O God, according to your unfailing love; according to your great compassion blot out my transgressions."

Thank you God for creating in me a pure heart. I know you are in me and me in you because I don't do the things I used to do. I don't think the way I used to think. Fasting has allowed me to see my sins and work diligently to minimize the desires of this world. I am still a work in progress. I can read and see myself in the Word. Thank you for the understanding.

Psalm 51:1 NIV

"A gentle answer turns away wrath, but a harsh word stirs up anger."

Lord, thank you for giving me a voice. I pray that every time I use it, my words are filled with sweet speech. Help me to use my voice to comfort and help others. Help me to avoid hurting those I care about. Fill my heart with good thoughts so that my thinking is nothing but uplifting towards others.

Proverbs 15:1 NIV

"Let us not become weary in doing good, for at the proper time we will reap a harvest if we do not give up. Therefore, as we have opportunity, let us do good to all people, especially to those who belong to the family of believers."

Lord, thank you for giving me the passion to help others. For providing me a grateful and forgiving spirit to do unto others as I would want to be treated.

Galatians 6:9-10 NIV

"In everything I did, I showed you that by this kind of hard work we must help the weak, remembering the words the Lord Jesus himself said: 'It is more blessed to give than to receive'."
Lord, create in me a pure heart; one that is full of love for those in need, and for all walks of life regardless of my personal bias. Continue to show me my gifts that are purposed for uplifting, motivating, and supporting others in and out of my circle of influence.
Acts 20:35 NIV

~~~~~~

"For we are God's handiwork, created in Christ Jesus to do good works, which God prepared in advance for us to do."
Thank you God for the good in me. For creating in me a pure heart filled with love; that in spite of trials and tribulations, I still have peace, and joy. Jesus, may your spirit continue to dwell in me so that my talk and my walk are aligned with your ways. Keep my thoughts from thinking evil when life's woes come my way. Instead, help me to find the strength to pray.
Ephesians 2:10 NIV

~~~~~~

"Make sure that nobody pays back wrong for wrong, but always strive to do what is good for each other and for everyone else."
Lord, thank you for your daily help and strength that provides me a forgiving heart to those who try to hurt and mistreat me. Continue to show me the good in things and people in spite of the evil that may exist. Give me a spirit of discernment that keeps me at a distance, helping if necessary from afar.
1 Thessalonians 5:15 NIV

"A gentle tongue [with its healing power] is a tree of life, but willful contrariness in it breaks down the spirit."
Lord, thank you in advance for giving me the right words to say. For helping me to not use my words for harm but instead for love and to help build up others. Thank you for cleaning my heart so that my words will speak truth, joy, peace, and life.
Proverbs 15:4 AMP

~~~~~

"Do not let any unwholesome talk come out of your mouths, but only what is helpful for building others up according to their needs, that it may benefit those who listen."
Lord, let the words of my mouth speak sweet words even to those people that say evil things to me. Regardless of the person, help me to use my words wisely. Give me words to uplift, just as I would want to be spoken to by others. Help me to speak words that will help and not harm. Amen.
Ephesians 4:29 NIV

~~~~~

"Be kind and compassionate to one another, forgiving each other, just as in Christ God forgave you."
Thank you God for giving me a forgiving spirit. Even when the ones that I love have angered and disappointed me. Although those times are etched in my mind, I thank you for helping me to not consume them in my heart, but instead provide me with peace and understanding.
Ephesians 4:32 NIV

"Whoever claims to love God yet hates a brother or sister is a liar. For whoever does not love their brother and sister, whom they have seen, cannot love God, whom they have not seen."

Oh God, please search my heart for any unforgiveness that may exist against another person. Create in me a pure heart that is absence of hate, malice, and evil. Fill it with love, joy, and forgiveness.

1 John 4:20 NIV

"Create in me a pure heart, O God, and renew a steadfast spirit within me."

Thank you God for working on my heart towards those who have offended me. I know you dwell in me and me in you because I don't respond and talk the way I used to before you delivered me. I don't think the way I used to think. But, I am still a work in progress. Thank you for opening my eyes so that I can see myself in Your Word. Hallelujah!

Psalm 51:10 NIV

"Make every effort to live in peace with everyone and to be holy; without holiness no one will see the Lord."

Lord, I thank you for showing me the power of prayer. For you have taught me that falling on my knees in prayer provides the peace that keeps me happy and confident in my daily walk, especially when the storms of life try to destroy my spirit. Your Word says, "I am holy because you are holy." So, I thank you for living in me, so that my reactions to the storms of life are with pure thoughts and love; creating peaceful thinking that assures me a place in the Kingdom. Hallelujah!

Hebrews 12:14 NIV

"He says, "Be still, and know that I am God; I will be exalted among the nations, I will be exalted in the earth."
Thank you God for taking care of my heart's desire. Thank you for showing me who you are by the awesome wonders and blessings you have allowed me to reap.
Psalm 46:10 NIV

"do not forget to do good and to share with others, for with such sacrifices God is pleased."
Thank You God for giving me a Spirit of giving and a heart for your people. Your Word says to treat others in the same way that I want to be treated. So Lord, daily I make an effort to say something nice, encourage or pay it forward with friends, family and even with strangers. Thank You God for opening my heart to even receive those who have not been so nice. I thank You also for a forgiving and peaceful heart. I love You Lord, and I love all people.
Hebrews 13:16 NIV

"Those who guard their lips preserve their lives, but those who speak rashly will come to ruin."
Lord God I pray let the words of my mouth be the meditation of my heart! Lord purify my heart, cleanse it from all evil thinking, so that my thoughts form words that speak praise, thanksgiving, joy and peace. Even when others speak on things that are not pleasing to me, I pray Lord that You will help me form words that are pleasing to You.
Proverbs 13:3 NIV

"Love the Lord your God with all your heart and with all your soul and with all your strength."
Lord God I love You, honor You, and will worship You forever with everything I am, and all that I have. My strength is because of You, and all that You promise to do. My heart is wide open to give and to receive. Because of You I can breathe. Thank You for my existence. Because of You I have peace, thank You for helping me to think clearly. Because of You I have courage, I can walk with my head up high and not in shame. It is because of You that I rejoice when others try to steal my joy.
Deuteronomy 6:5 NIV

~~~~~

"For we are God's handiwork, created in Christ Jesus to do good works, which God prepared in advance for us to do."
Thank You God for creating in me the Spirit of goodness; providing me a heart that shows compassion for those less fortunate. Daily I pray that my walk and my talk are aligned with Your Will, and that You are pleased with me. Thank You for sending the Holy Spirit to remind me when my heart gets crushed; how I handle the pain is to give it to You and trust. I admit that sometimes my heart and mind do not align, thank You for Your love and forgiveness each and every time.
Ephesians 2:10 NIV

His Word and His Way

"Because I said so!" How many times have we heard that statement from our parents? How many times have we said it to our children? Their way, or our way, was sometimes good advice. But, honestly, it was not always the best advice. The best way to follow is God's way. I have graduated from high school, and went on to earn three degrees; by society's standards, I have done well. However, spiritually, I had left God out of the little things in my life. I left Him out of my finances, health, relationships, and sometimes my daily interactions with people. As ridiculous as it may sound, I didn't think God needed to be bothered with the small stuff! In actuality, I needed Him and His guidance with every word I spoke, every place I traveled, with every person I encountered, with every job I held, and every moment I walk this earth.

It wasn't that my life was a complete mess, but I realized that life without God's guidance was like not living at all. I used God's Word to restore my mind, give me sound thinking, create a sweet taste in my mouth. Even for my enemies, I wanted my words to be words of love, joy, and to provide comfort. I used His Word to clean me from the inside out, so that my body would be full of life and energy to do a good work for God and His people. I wanted to please God. I wanted to make Him happy.

The Bible says to be doers of the Word; to not just hear the Word. It is our actions that tell the story about our character, motivation, and commitment. God's Word and His Way are the only way to righteous living. My inner man had to align with my outer man, so that I could present all of me for fixing.

Proverbs 13:10 tells us, "Where there is strife, there is pride, but wisdom is found in those who take advice." I realized that if I asked fifty different people for advice that the advice given would not provide what I needed from one person....God. So when I began to move forward and think ahead, I prayed for God to lead me in the way He would have me to go. To provide me the ability to discern the thoughts of others, so that my direction remained aligned with His Will and His Way. To keep me from evil on my new journey, He began to open my ears so that I could hear Him clearly. Even in the midst of confusion, to help me to seek out his guidance.

Whose voice are you listening to? Is it directing you on a path of peace, joy, and happiness?

How do you honor His Will and His Way?

"And whatever you do, whether in word or deed, do it all in the name of the Lord Jesus, giving thanks to God the Father through him."
Let my walk be your walk. My mind be your mind. My talk be like your talk. Thank you Jesus for being with me, for teaching and showing me your ways. You are such a good role model. I love you and forever thank you.
Colossians 3:17 NIV

"Teach me to do your will, for you are my God; may your good Spirit lead me on level ground."
I pray that my walk is your walk. Open my eyes and my ears to see and hear the things that you would have me to know. Guide me in a way that allows me to grow in you. Consume my mind with good thoughts which speak to my heart, that I may always remember to praise you in spite of….
Psalm 143:10 NIV

"Whatever you do, work at it with all your heart, as working for the Lord, not for human masters, since you know that you will receive an inheritance from the Lord as a reward. It is the Lord Christ you are serving."
Everything I do Lord, I do for You and in Your name. You are the reason I get up each morning, and for that I am forever grateful. My prayer is to walk and talk in total alignment with Your Word; fasting and praying that I receive the blessings You have promised me. Continue to show me my wrongs so that I can make them right. Thank you God for Your glorious light.
Colossians 3:23 NIV

"For the word of God is alive and active. Sharper than any double-edged sword, it penetrates even to dividing soul and spirit, joints and marrow; it judges the thoughts and attitudes of the heart."
Thank you Lord for Your Word and providing me the understanding which allows me to see myself in it. I pray for strength daily to be able to spend the time reading to get to know You. The Word keeps me grounded in what I think, say, and do! It helps me focus on how I am supposed to please You. Thank you for the sound teaching that guides my thinking.
Hebrews 4:12 NIV

"With man this is impossible, but not with God; all things are possible with God."
Thank you for the reminder that I can do all things through you. You are my light and my compass who helps guide my walk and talk. If only I give you full reign to take charge over me.
Mark 10:27 NIV

"Whoever believes in me, as Scripture has said, rivers of living water will flow from within them."
Lord, not only do I believe in you, I live for you and love you with all my heart! I know my life would be a lot different without you living inside of me. I am grateful for your presence and stand in awe often when your Word comes to life in my walk towards salvation. Thank you for the overflow.
John 7:38 NIV

"But just as he who called you is holy, so be holy in all you do; for it is written: "Be holy, because I am holy."
Once again, thank you Lord for the sound instruction in your Word. I have learned that being "holy" is not negative, but is one who is diligently seeking to do and be a person of good character! I pray that my walk and my talk represent you!
1 Peter 1:15-16 NIV

"Jesus answered, "It is written: 'Man shall not live on bread alone, but on every word that comes from the mouth of God.'"
Hallelujah! Thank you God for your Word! For providing us a blueprint in advance on our purpose in this life. Your Word in Genesis tells us that we are "good," so Lord, help us to walk and talk that way. I rebuke those who try to tell us something different. Thank you for Your Word that helps to satisfy my appetite, filling me up with joy, peace, wisdom, and thanksgiving! Thank you.
Matthew 4:4 NIV

"Dear children, let us not love with words or speech but with actions and in truth."
The Bible says to be doers of the Word; to not just hear the Word. It is our actions that tell the story about our character, motivation, and commitment. Transparency is the key to a pure heart, mind, body, and soul. Thank you God for the truth in your Word.
1 John 3:18 NIV

"Dear friends, do not believe every spirit, but test the spirits to see whether they are from God, because many false prophets have gone out into the world."

Thank you God in advance for giving me the gift of discernment. For showing me who you are in my life so that I stay true to your Will and your Way.

1 John 4:1 NIV

"Whoever loves discipline loves knowledge, but whoever hates correction is stupid."

Thank you God for using your Word to teach me the way to go. To learn the things that keep me wise in you and how I should walk, talk, and how I should treat others who are in my life. Thank you for showing me how to handle corrective criticism and using my mistakes to make wiser decisions.

Proverbs 12:1 NIV

"But if we walk in the light, as he is in the light, we have fellowship with one another, and the blood of Jesus, his Son, purifies us from all sin."

Thank you Lord for Your guiding light! It reminds me to align my daily walk with Your Will and Your way. Your light reminds me to stay connected to like-minded people, and to let go of those who engage in 'stinking thinking.' Your light shines bright; it opens my heart and mind to give and to receive, and to love and to forgive. Thank you for Your light; it purifies my heart and my soul

1 John 1:7 NIV

"Make every effort to live in peace with everyone and to be holy; without holiness no one will see the Lord."
Lord, I thank you for showing me the power of prayer. For you have taught me that prayer provides the peace that keeps me confident in my daily walk, when others try to destroy my spirit. I thank you for living in me, so that I treat those same people with love, creating peaceful relationships.
Hebrews 12:14 NIV

"so Christ was sacrificed once to take away the sins of many; and he will appear a second time, not to bear sin, but to bring salvation to those who are waiting for him."
Thank You God for the sacrifice! Thank You Jesus for bearing my burdens and bearing the sins of this world so that we could live free. I pray that I am worthy of Your attention when You return. Every day, I try to make every effort to live a life that is pleasing to Your sight. I am not perfect, but this You already know. I am walking in faith and putting my trust in You.
Hebrews 9:28 NIV

"I will instruct you and teach you in the way you should go; I will counsel you with my loving eye on you."
Thank you God for your commitment to be my teacher. To show me how to walk, where to walk, and what to pay attention to on my journey. I am forever grateful to you for choosing me to guide through this crazy world called life.
Psalm 32:8 NIV

"May the God of hope fill you with all joy and peace as you trust in him, so that you may overflow with hope by the power of the Holy Spirit."
Thank You Lord! Hope, peace, and joy are what I pray for each day. I will trust in you always, and do my best to be Obedient Your Will and Your Way. Thank You for providing the presence of the Holy Spirit, who provides me with subtle reminders each day. I hope that my days are long and my troubles are few, I am relying on You Lord to carry my burdens with You. In the midst of my trials, I hope that my mind stays focused on You, I am relying on You Lord to make all
things new.
Romans 15:13 NIV

~~~~~

"for it is God who works in you to will and to act in order to fulfill his good purpose."
Thank You God for Your presence that is within me. I am not sure of the person I would be, if You didn't send Your son to die on the cross at Calvary. I know it is You who keeps my emotions contained when others mess with me, thank you for holding my tongue, so that my reactions come in peace. There have been so many times when I wanted to do things my own way, thank You for sending the Holy Spirit to whisper that it was not ok. You have saved me from myself so many times I can't count, I am so glad You love me without any doubts. I pray that my heart stays open to receive all of You, Lord please continue to show me my purpose, so that my ways are aligned with You. I am praying circles around some things in my life that I want to come true, thank You God for showing me how to have complete faith in You!
Philippians 2:13 NIV

"Nothing in all creation is hidden from God's sight. Everything is uncovered and laid bare before the eyes of him to whom we must give account."

Oh Lord, I pray that everything I do and say are pleasing in Your sight. I pray that my daily interactions with others are committed in joy, peace, and thanksgiving. I pray for a disappearance of all known and unknown weaknesses that cause me to sin against You! Purify my heart with forgiveness for those situations from the past, and those that exist today, so that my heart is free of pain and anger, and opened up to give and receive love even when I have been offended. I know that what is done in the dark will eventually be seen in the light, so I pray that You guide my daily walk in and through the light. And when that day comes to join You in the home above, I pray that I am welcomed as Your good and faithful servant.

Hebrews 4:13 NIV

~~~~~

"Endure hardship as discipline; God is treating you as his children. For what children are not disciplined by their father?"

Oh Lord I pray daily for the strength to stand strong in the trials and tribulations of this life. Thank You for holding me accountable for those things that do not align with Your Word, and showing me by Your presence that You truly care about me. Lord continue to show me myself, continue to purify my heart so that it is open to forgive, and Lord please continue to give me good thoughts so that my words encourage, bring joy and speak love.

Hebrews 12:7 NIV

"Trust in the Lord with all your heart and lean not on your own understanding; in all your ways submit to him, and he will make your paths straight."

Oh Lord, I hope You know how much I love, honor, worship, and trust Your presence in my life. You are so worthy to be praised for all of the blessings that You have allowed me to reap; even when I was not deserving. Thank You for Your Grace. Yes, there are times when I think I have the answers and I move to fast. I often have to circle back around to You for help to complete the task. I am grateful for the Holy Spirit who always gives me that feeling when my decisions are all me, he reminds me that I don't have to do it alone, that there is always a We! With You Lord I know everything is possible, obtainable, reachable, and doable! I will make every effort to follow Your Will and Your Way. Thank You for having my back when others do not. Thank You for bearing my burdens when they are too much to handle. Thank You Lord for Your everlasting care.

Proverbs 3:5-6 NIV

Total Praise

I cannot say that I have had a terrible life. But, I have had my share of many chaotic moments. I grew up attending the Catholic Church, but I am not sure I had a relationship with God. Truthfully, there was no relationship with God; I did not know who He was or His power. When chaos arose during my early years of being a wife and mother, I either kept secrets, or damned the God that I didn't know for my circumstances. In 1996/1997, I began attending Faith Deliverance Pentecostal Church. Pastor Davis taught me more about God in three months than I had learned in three years attending a mega church! One of the most important things I learned during this time was about praising God in, around, and during my circumstance.

If I allowed my circumstances to control my thoughts, actions and reactions, I am not sure if I would be a live today. My mantra was and still is, "God thank you for my trials and tribulations that I am going through. Please give me the strength to go through with joy in my heart and peace on my mind. Thank you Lord for loving me." I also became a reader of 1 Thessalonians 5:16--
"Rejoice always, pray continually, give thanks in all

circumstances; for this is God's will for you in Christ Jesus." Through the good, the bad, in sickness, and in good health, praising God is what we must do! Colossians 3:17 (NIV), tells us to do whatever we do; in word or deed, all in the name of the Lord Jesus. I am a witness, He will not bring you to a situation that He cannot bring you through. I have learned over time to give Him all of the credit for everything I say and do. I praise Him, I honor and I began to put my total trust in Him! Our trials are just set-ups for breakthroughs of peace and prosperity.

Praising God in the good times as well as the bad times is so important. Praising Him when life gets tough is so critical to our deliverance. I learned that I had to keep a steady praise in my mind and in my heart in order to stay sane during the chaos moments occurring in my life. I praised in tears, I praised in song, and I intentionally praised Him in laughter to keep my mind thinking of His goodness in spite of the sadness I was really feeling. When we praise God in all of circumstances, His presence is full of love. I thank God for keeping me in His Will. How often do you praise God?

How do you praise God in in the midst of your circumstances?

"My mouth is filled with your praise, declaring your splendor all day long."
Lord, I am careful to always speak good of you and how you take care of me. I know that when I praise you it still does not show my full gratitude.
Psalm 71:8 NIV

~~~~~

"I love you, Lord, my strength. The Lord is my rock, my fortress and my deliverer; my God is my rock, in whom I take refuge, my shield and the horn of my salvation, my stronghold."
Thank you Lord for being my everything. When I can't count on family and friends, I know all I have to do is just call your name. Thank you for being my soul mate and lifetime partner!
Psalm 18:1-2 NIV

~~~~~

"For his anger lasts only a moment, but his favor lasts a lifetime; weeping may stay for the night, but rejoicing comes in the morning."
Thank you God for your constant love. So much that you would allow my sorrows to be shortened just to a days' time. Thank you for providing me comfort and helping me to see the joy in the midst of my pain.
Psalm 30:5 NIV

"But blessed is the one who trusts in the lord, whose confidence is in him. They will be like a tree planted by the water that sends out its roots by the stream. It does not fear when heat comes; its leaves are always green. It has no worries in a year of drought and never fails to bear fruit."

Thank you Jesus for being a man that I can put my total trust in. For being reliable, trustworthy and dependable. It is because of you that I rest in total faith that my storms will turn into sunshine.

Jeremiah 17:7 NIV

"Until now you have not asked for anything in my name. Ask and you will receive, and your joy will be complete."

Thank you Lord! Man requires so much more for use of a name! To know that I can just call out Yours and my life results in joy is an awesome feeling! Oh, the blessings of a name! Thank you for the comfort, for the peace, for the love. I promise not to use it in vain.

John 16:24 NIV

"But, 'Let the one who boasts boast in the Lord.' For it is not the one who commends himself who is approved, but the one whom the Lord commends."

I pray that I am worthy enough to be commended by You Lord! Everything I do, I am careful to give you praise and honor. I do not take any credit, but give it all to You, for all that I am and all that I have been able to do.

2 Corinthians 10:17-18 NIV

> "Come, let us sing for joy to the Lord; let us shout aloud to the Rock of our salvation. Let us come before him with thanksgiving and extol him with music and song."

Lord, I love You and will praise Your name all the days of my life. Exalting Your name with a loud voice, I will sing of Your love and kindness. Thank you for loving me, saving me, and creating a good work in me!

Psalm 95:1-2 NIV

> "But those who hope in the Lord will renew their strength. They will soar on wings like eagles; they will run and not grow weary, they will walk and not be faint."

Thank you, Lord! I am so glad that I have put my trust in You and not in man! I hope, I believe, I honor, and I trust in You with all my heart. Thank you for the strength; it helps me deal with the daily challenges and obstacles I encounter, directly and indirectly. Thank you for Your peace; it gives me a sound mind to think on those things wise and good. Thank you for just being God! Hallelujah!

Isaiah 40:31 NIV

> "For I am not ashamed of the gospel, because it is the power of God that brings salvation to everyone who believes: first to the Jew, then to the Gentile."

Lord, you are my everything. There is none like you! I will speak of your goodness all the days of my life, even during times of pain and suffering. You are great!

Romans 1:16 NIV

"In that day you will say: "Give praise to the Lord, proclaim his name; make known among the nations what he has done, and proclaim that his name is exalted. Sing to the Lord, for he has done glorious things; let this be known to all the world."

Lord, I will speak of your goodness all the days of my life. I praise you for my joy as well as my pain. I am so thankful for Your love of protection. You know just what I need and your presence is always right on time. Thank you for taking charge over my mind, body, and soul.

Isaiah 12:4-5 NIV

"Enter his gates with thanksgiving and his courts with praise; give thanks to him and praise his name. For the Lord is good and his love endures forever; his faithfulness continues through all generations."

Lord, I am always mindful to thank you for all that you do! Even during times of chaos in my life, I thank you for seeing me through. You have been my constant companion who has loved me, especially on the days when I didn't love myself, and those days when others took advantage of my love. Thank you for letting me stand in the gap for others in my life who are still trying to figure You out. I give praise to Your name.

Psalm 100:4-5 NIV

"Be glad, people of Zion, rejoice in the Lord your God, for he has given you the autumn rains because he is faithful. He sends you abundant showers, both autumn and spring rains, as before."
Lord, I will rejoice in You all the days of my life. Always remembering what blessings You have provided me, even when I didn't deserve to receive. Thank you for keeping my dark days short and always bringing light to the challenges in my life.
Joel 2:23 NIV

~~~~~

"Give praise to the Lord, proclaim his name; make known among the nations what he has done."
Thank you God for your grace and mercy. All that I have and all that I am, I owe it to you! I am not ashamed to speak about your goodness and love. Every chance I get, I will brag about the many times you have fought my battles by removing the thorns that try to steal my joy, take my peace, and contaminate my body. I am forever grateful!
1 Chronicles 16:8 NIV

~~~~~

"Be kind and compassionate to one another, forgiving each other, just as in Christ God forgave you."
Thank you God for giving me a forgiving spirit, even when the ones that I love have angered and disappointed me. Although those times are etched in my mind, I thank you for helping me to not consume them in my heart, but instead provide me with peace and understanding.
Ephesians 4:32 NIV

"And everyone who calls on the name of the Lord will be saved."

Your name: the all-powerful, all knowing, savior, redeemer, deliverer, there is so much to Your name! Thank You Lord for making freedom just that easy, with just the utterance of Your name. I will call Your name daily. I will be careful not to use it in vain, but use it to provide me comfort, peace and joy. I pray that family and friends know how to call on Your name during their good and bad days, and when they call, that You would honor them with blessings beyond their imaginations.

Acts 2:21 NIV

"But you are a chosen people, a royal priesthood, a holy nation, God's special possession, that you may declare the praises of him who called you out of darkness into his wonderful light."

Thank You God for choosing me to walk in Your marvelous light. I honor and adore You for teaching me how to live right. Your Word teaches me how to get back up when the evil of this world tries to knock me down, comfort, peace and joy, in Your Word I have found. Through sickness, chaos, and trials & tribulations, because of Your light, Your Word has revealed holy revelations. I praise You and honor You because Your Word continuously renews my thinking, when life presents me with challenges, it is Your Word that keeps me from stinking thinking. Thank You Holy Spirit for reminding me to walk in faith with kingdom principles, I put all my trust in You, because with You all things are possible. Thank You for the strength to pray circles around my dreams and hopes for the future, No weapon formed against me shall prosper!

1Peter 2:9 NIV

"Give praise to the lord, proclaim his name; make known among the nations what he has done."
Thank you God for the big and small blessings. For providing favor even in those times I didn't deserve it. I realize that everything I am is not because of what I have done, but because of you operating in me. I give you glory and honor, and will forever praise your name.
Psalm 105:1 NIV

"And whatever you do, whether in word or deed, do it all in the name of the Lord Jesus, giving thanks to God the Father through him."
Lord God everything I do, how I do it, why I do it, and when I do it, I try my best so that It pleases You! Every day I pray for strength to walk in Your Will and Your Way. I have to be honest and You already know, my flesh takes over sometimes preventing my spiritual growth. Self takes over and my patience is short, although the Holy Spirit speaks, I disregard what has been taught. I have learned over time to give You all the credit for everything I say and do, I praise You, I honor and put my total trust in You! I thank You for every blessing I have received, especially the ones that I didn't think I needed. I thank You and I love You for You being You!
Colossians 3:17 NIV

"How great you are, Sovereign Lord! There is no one like you, and there is no God but you, as we have heard with our own ears."

Lord God how great is Your name and worthy to be praised! Surely I will never forget about You and all that You have done for me. You sacrificed Your Son just for me! You are the Alpha and the Omega; no man has ever been greater. You are my joy, peace and happiness; please don't leave me Lord, Your presence I would miss. You are my rock, and my strength comes from You, thank You for Favor because I put all my trust In You. You cleared my mind and purified my heart, from You Lord I shall never depart.

2 Samuel 7:22 NIV

~~~~~

"For our light and momentary troubles are achieving for us an eternal glory that far outweighs them all. So we fix our eyes not on what is seen, but on what is unseen, since what is seen is temporary, but what is unseen is eternal."

Oh Lord, thank You for Your light that continues to shine bright through my good and bad moments. I feel so thankful for the blessings that are to come. It is so good to know that my today's woes will not be my tomorrow's problems. Thank You God for Your constant attention on what I say and do. Thank You Lord for Your goodness and Your mercy. Thank You for purifying my heart daily so that my thoughts are renewed and focused on what is good and not on what is evil. Thank You for the strength to stand strong in faith, waiting in expectancy for You to make all things new. Lord I thank You and honor You for Your Love; Your love that makes everything alright, always possible, and always on time.

2 Corinthians 4:17-18 NIV

"For it is not the one who commends himself who is approved, but the one whom the Lord commends."
Oh Lord continue to show me how to be in Your perfect Will. Please forgive me of any self-righteous talk or ways that may deny You from getting the glory. I pray that You see me worthy enough to keep Your light shining through me, so that it is You Lord that gets the glory and honor. I pray for a humbled Spirit, absent of selfishness, and self-serving ideology.
2 Corinthians 10:18 NIV

~~~~~

"For we must all appear before the judgment seat of Christ, so that each of us may receive what is due us for the things done while in the body, whether good or bad."
Oh Lord I pray that when the time comes, I can stand before You transformed from my old ways. I pray that I am standing completely purified. A clean heart, with good thoughts, and a soul completely sold out for You. Lord, if by chance you catch me on a bad day, I pray that my good days out weigh my bad days
2 Corinthians 5:10 NIV

Perfect Peace

You can't learn courage until you know fear. Well, at least that is my experience. I feared man, advancement, success, happiness, death, and life itself. Fear would have such a strong grip on me that it created self-doubt, even in the things that I was most comfortable in and with. Fear paralyzed me. Fear took away my courage and caused me to keep secrets and tell lies. Finding the courage to overcome it was key to my living successfully. The key to finding the courage to overcome fear was having faith in Him! As I spent time in God's Word, I realized that fear and faith did not mix. They are like oil and water; when faith kicks in, fear moves out, and they become two separate entities. I sank deeper in the Word of God, and rested in His peace instead of my fear. In Proverbs 1:33, God tells us that if we would just listen to Him that He would keep us safe and we would live without fear of harm.

Living in perfect peace seems unrealistic, but with God all things are possible. He says if we just rest in him, he will take care of all of our needs. I realized that I had to give God full reign over my life so that I could have an opportunity to feel perfect peace. I was excited and looked forward to experiencing a sense of tranquility in my life.

My friend, Katrina Miller, lived her life in perfect peace. She felt pain throughout her body because of cancer; however, Katrina was able to provide words of comfort while she was in pain and in the midst of her cancer storm. She embodied peace by her actions and by her words of comfort for everyone else while she suffered in pain. Through Katrina, I learned that living in perfect peace means to thank God for His purpose regardless of our situations, and to rejoice even in our worst moments.

Jesus says, "Come to me if you are tired and burdened. I'll make your load lighter, and help you carry your burden." Jesus offers us rest amidst the stress! He invites us to allow Him to help us handle the stressors that come daily. He does not mind facing our daily challenges with us. Allowing Him to walk with you daily, trusting Him for guidance and wisdom to handle whatever comes, is the way to experience peace in the midst of the storm. I am still learning, what about you? How do you create tranquil moments during your day with others who stir up chaos and confusion?

How do you create and find perfect peace:

"And with your feet fitted with the readiness that comes from the gospel of peace."
Lord, thank you for peace even in the midst of the storm. Thank you for giving me a steadfast focus even when evil tries to come my way. Thank you for giving me a mind that knows how to call on Your name in the time of need.
Ephesians 6:15 NIV

"I rejoiced greatly in the Lord that at last you renewed your concern for me. Indeed, you were concerned, but you had no opportunity to show it."
Thank you Lord in advance for fulfilling my every need, causing me to be satisfied with what you have saw fit for me to be blessed with. I thank you in advance for total satisfaction in You who has supplied all of my needs.
Philippians 4:10 NIV

"Let the peace of Christ rule in your hearts, since as members of one body you were called to peace. And be thankful."
Thank you God for your gift of peace. That even in the midst of my storms, you allow me to walk through with a sweet and quiet spirit. When others try to provoke me in rage, you provide me with a sweet taste so that my words are direct but said in love. Continue to show me how to think peace, and be the peace, as I go through my everyday trials and tribulations.
Colossians 3:15 NIV

"Truly my soul finds rest in God; my salvation comes from him."
Lord, I thank you for allowing me to rest in your arms when I need comfort from life's woes. It is there where I feel the most safe, and the most loved. It is because of You that peace rests in my heart, even when my life feels like it is spinning out of control. Thank you God for your protection.
Psalm 62:1 NIV

"He who earnestly seeks after and craves righteousness, mercy, and loving-kindness will find life in addition to righteousness (uprightness and right standing with God) and honor."
Thank you God for the energy and the desire to seek good things that honor you in my sometimes chaotic life.
Proverbs 21:21 AMP

"Peacemakers who sow in peace reap a harvest of righteousness."
God, thank you in advance for providing me peace even in the midst of chaos. For your spirit that speaks within me when my words are hard to say.
James 3:18 NIV

"Give praise to the lord, proclaim his name; make known among the nations what he has done."
Thank you God for the big and small blessings. For providing favor even in those times when I was undeserving. I realize that everything I am, is not what I have done, but because of you operating in me. I give you glory and honor, and will forever praise your name.

Psalm 105:1 NIV
"Set your minds on things above, not on earthly things."
Lord, thank you for the reminder of what's to come. Eternal peace and eternal life. I pray for focused direction and Your guidance to help me discern those things, people and places that contradict my goal to live in the Kingdom.
Colossians 3:2 NIV

~~~~~

"Be joyful in hope, patient in affliction, faithful in prayer."
Lord, thank you for giving me strength while dealing with the chaos in my life. I will not complain as I go through, but instead will pray for peace in my heart, and joy in my spirit during the midst of these storms. Your Word says joy comes in the morning, and so Lord I will wait on You to deliver the blessings that are stored up for me to receive. I have hope, and stand in expectation that You will do just what You say You are going to do! Hallelujah!
Romans 12:12 NIV

~~~~~

"Let the peace of Christ rule in your hearts, since as members of one body you were called to peace. And be thankful."
Thank you God for your gift of peace. That even in the midst of my storms, you allow me to walk through with a sweet and quiet spirit. When others try to provoke me in rage, you provide me with a sweet taste so that my words are direct but said in love. Continue to show me how to think peace and be the peace as I go through my everyday trials and tribulations.
Colossians 3:15 NIV

"You will keep in perfect peace those whose minds are steadfast, because they trust in you."
Lord, you have taught me and shown me over and over the value of possessing a faithful spirit. I have vowed to remain faithful to your way. I am so thankful to you for showing me how to find peace in my mind, for my body, and my spirit. Thank you for giving me perfect peace in the midst of my storms.
Isaiah 26:3 NIV

"I rejoiced greatly in the Lord that at last you renewed your concern for me. Indeed, you were concerned, but you had no opportunity to show it. I am not saying this because I am in need, for I have learned to be content whatever the circumstances."
Lord, I thank you in advance for total satisfaction in You who has already supplied my wants and desires. I have faith in your word. Thank you for my health, my finances, and all the blessings that you see fit for me to reap. Thank you for being my comforter when I feel alone, hurt, and misunderstood; for strength when I am feeling weak.
Philippians 4:10 NIV

"Peace I leave with you; my peace I give you. I do not give to you as the world gives. Do not let your hearts be troubled and do not be afraid."
Thank You Lord Jesus for providing Your peace. Because of Your peace I can be free to be me. Because of Your peace, I believe No weapon formed against me shall prosper. I will not fear man, and I will not fear change. I know there will be trials, but I thank You
in advance for giving me a peace that keeps my mind focused, my heart content, and my feet planted on solid ground. Thank You for the peace that protects comforts and gives joy.
John 14:27 NIV

~~~~~

"And the peace of God, which transcends all understanding, will guard your hearts and your minds in Christ Jesus."
Thank you God for Your everlasting peace; peace in my heart, and peace in my mind. At times it is difficult to avoid the feelings that often come from being angry, frustrated, disappointed, anxious, and impatient. My carnal thinking wants to kill, destroy and retaliate. But thanks be to You the God that loves me unconditionally! When chaos arises, You send the Holy Spirit to comfort me. Your Word reminds me of Your greatest sacrifice, and the peace upon Your Son when He died up on the cross to pay the price for our sins. How dare I not be at peace! God I pray that family and friends find the peace that they may be searching for. I pray that for some, in spite of the realities of health issues, inadequate finances, job related stresses, and failed relationships & friendships, Your PEACE must be sought and achieved!
Philippians 4:7 NIV

2 Peter 3:9 NIV "The Lord is not slow in keeping his promise, as some understand slowness. Instead he is patient with you, not wanting anyone to perish, but everyone to come to repentance."
Thank you Lord for Your perfect timing. You always know just what I need and when I need it. Thank You for being patient with my sometimes slow response to Your Word. I am so grateful that You see my heart, and know that I try my best to live according to Your precepts daily. Lord I pray that You continue to bless me with the same patience for others who may be slow in their actions and reactions. Give me peace and understanding of Your timing while You bring clarity to their minds. Thank You God for Your patience with me!
2 Peter 3:9 NIV

~~~~~~

"But he was pierced for our transgressions, he was crushed for our iniquities; the punishment that brought us peace was on him, and by his wounds we are healed."
Lord God, thank You for sending Your Son Jesus to die up on the cross for the sins of this world. You made the ultimate sacrifice just so little ole me could live free. Because of You I have peace when the space around me is chaotic. Because of You I have joy in the midst of sadness and pain. Because of You I am strong even when life's challenges make me weak. Because of You all things are new, so I have a forgiving heart that does not dwell in the past where others have hurt me or let me down. Because of You I can stand tall in times of adversity because Your Word picks me up when I fall down. It is all because of Your love Lord, I love all people for who they are, and not hate because of how they treat me. Because of Your goodness, grace & mercy, I am who I am, and not who I used to be. Thank You Lord for saving me! Hallelujah!
Isaiah 53:5 NIV

Grateful

My grandmother always taught us that we were supposed to be grateful for everything that we had, especially because we were being raised by a single mother. We often heard: "Don't waste food. Be happy with what you have, because there are many that don't even have what we have." I can remember sitting at my grandma's kitchen table for hours trying to digest soggy corn flakes. She refused to allow me to throw them in the trash. Those days and many others taught me to be grateful for the food, clothes, and shelter that my mom struggled to provide.

As an adult, I learned that it is the gift of knowing God that I would one day be grateful for before all else! It is so easy to take life for granted, and have no clue what gifts each of us have been blessed with by God's grace. We become self-centered and only concerned with what we want, how we want it, and how quick we can get it. We often forget about the people who genuinely suffer from inadequacies, poor self-esteem, and illness. Someone always has it worse than you. Through God's Word, He teaches us to be content with what we have, and most importantly, to be content with Him.

Daily Spiritual Nugget

My friend Cassandra taught me about being grateful. She often would remind me about living a short life when I complained about my trials and tribulations. She would say "those are small trials compared to my mine." She was so right! She was a 36-year-old beautiful wife and mother of three, and she was dying. How dare I complain? Cassandra would never see her children become adults. She would miss graduations, marriages, birthdays, and grandchildren. Why was I complaining?

I am grateful for His presence during the chaotic moments in my life, because it is He who provided me strength. His presence has kept me sane, comforted, and at peace. I am so very grateful for his Word. I have used it to cleanse me from evil, and to guide me to live a holy and acceptable life in God's eyes. I am forever grateful to God for opening my eyes to His Will and His Way. Because of Him, I am free. I am blessed. I am rich.

What about you? What are you the most grateful for? Are you complaining about life, or are you living life with God's presence?

What are you most grateful for?

_____

_____

_____

_____

_____

_____

_____

_____

_____

_____

_____

_____

_____

_____

_____

_____

_____

_____

"Therefore, rid yourselves of all malice and all deceit, hypocrisy, envy, and slander of every kind."
Thank you for choosing me. I am so thankful and grateful. Thank you for the stamina to do good, to be obedient to you, and to use my body as a living sacrifice. I know I am loved and because of that, I am forever grateful for your love.
1 Peter 2:1 NIV

"Enter his gates with thanksgiving and his courts with praise; give thanks to him and praise his name."
Thank you, God. Thank you for allowing me to minister to Your people. For allowing me to speak Your Words. My prayer from this day forth is to ask You for what I want. I have learned to speak things into existence and let it go. Thank you for today. My prayers were answered! Thank you for providing me with a pleasant day doing what makes me happy! I Love you God with all my heart!
Psalm 100:4 NIV

"I love the Lord, for he heard my voice; he heard my cry for mercy. Because he turned his ear to me, I will call on him as long as I live."
Lord, I pray that you know how much I really love you! I am thankful every day for your love, and the time you take to listen to my war cry. You have delivered me from harm's way, given me peace during the chaos, made me feel strong during my weakest moments, and provided me wisdom when I just didn't understand! I am forever grateful to you. Thank you.
Psalm 116:1-2 NIV

"A new command I give you: Love one another. As I have loved you, so you must love one another. By this everyone will know that you are my disciples, if you love one another."

Thank you God for giving me a servant's heart. Teaching and showing me how to love thy neighbor regardless of biological connection. To love others even when I don't feel loved back.

John 13:34-35 NIV

~~~~~

"For the Spirit God gave us does not make us timid, but gives us power, love and self-discipline."

Thank you God for allowing your spirit to dwell within me, which makes me feel courageous during times of adversity, strong during weak moments, and wise when faced with confusion. I am grateful for Your peace when chaos arises. Thank you!

2 Timothy 1:7 NIV

~~~~~

"So do not fear, for I am with you; do not be dismayed, for I am your God. I will strengthen you and help you; I will uphold you with my righteous right hand."

Thank you God for standing with me in times of trouble. For healing the sickness in my body and in my mind. I am so glad that I can count on you when others turn their backs. I am forever grateful to you for turning my sorrows into joy and my chaos into peace. I love you Lord!

Isaiah 41:10 NIV

"I will instruct you and teach you in the way you should go; I will counsel you with my loving eye on you."
Thank you God for your commitment to be my teacher. To show me how to walk, where to walk, and what to pay attention to on my journey. I am forever grateful to you for choosing me to guide through this unpredictable world.
Psalm 32:8 NIV

"Let us not become weary in doing good, for at the proper time we will reap a harvest if we do not give up. Therefore, as we have opportunity, let us do good to all people, especially to those who belong to the family of believers."
Lord, thank you for giving me the passion to help others. For providing me a grateful and forgiving spirit to do unto others as I would want to be treated.
Galatians 6:9-10 NIV

"For Christ's love compels us, because we are convinced that one died for all, and therefore all died. And he died for all, that those who live should no longer live for themselves but for him who died for them and was raised again."
Thank you for the ultimate sacrifice just for me. When you died for me, you gave me an opportunity to live and be free from sin. I owe my life to you, and as a result, I promise to do my best to be an example of who You are. To live through you, to talk and walk through you!
2 Corinthians 5-14 NIV

"Whatever you do, work at it with all your heart, as working for the Lord, not for human masters, since you know that you will receive an inheritance from the Lord as a reward. It is the Lord Christ you are serving."
Everything I do Lord, I do for You and in Your name. You are the reason I get up each morning, and for that I am forever grateful. My prayer is to walk and talk in total alignment with Your Word; fasting and praying that I receive the blessings You have promised me. Continue to show me my wrongs so that I can make them right. Thank you God for Your glorious light.
Colossians 3:23 NIV

"Do not judge, or you too will be judged."
Lord, please forgive me if I have spoken ill of or demeaned another for their physical, emotional, or social being. My words are not meant to be judgmental, but hopeful for Kingdom living. Only You can judge the fate of people! I am very thankful for what You have allowed me to accomplish, and grateful for all of the blessings You have allowed me to reap.
Matthew 7:1 NIV

"But thanks be to God! He gives us the victory through our Lord Jesus Christ."
Lord, thank you for your son and your sacrifice through his death on the cross. For allowing Him to bear the burden of my sins, I am forever grateful for your generosity in love. Because of your love, I am free in my mind and in my spirit!
1 Timothy 4:8 NIV

"Love the Lord your God with all your heart and with all your soul and with all your strength."
Lord God I love You, honor You, and will worship You forever with everything I am, and all that I have. My strength is because of You, and all that You promise to do. My heart is wide open to give and to receive. Because of You I can breathe. Thank You for my existence. Because of You I have peace, thank You for helping me to think clearly. Because of You I have courage, I can walk with my head up high and not in shame. It is because of You that I rejoice when others try to steal my joy.
Deuteronomy 6:5 NIV

"Very truly I tell you, whoever hears my word and believes him who sent me has eternal life and will not be judged but has crossed over from death to life."
Thank You God for Your Word I am a witness that it provided comfort from pain, heals the mind and body, brings joy in the morning, and peace that is everlasting. I believe that You will do what You say You will do, so I stand in expectation for Your promises. Thank You for the opportunity to live.
John 5:24 NIV

"May the God of hope fill you with all joy and peace as you trust in him, so that you may overflow with hope by the power of the Holy Spirit."
Oh Lord, I pray daily to be filled with Your Spirit. Help me to consume my thoughts with peace and joy. Even when chaos arises in my life; at work, at home, and with family and friends, I pray that Your Spirit speaks through me so that my actions and reactions are aligned with Your Will and Your Way. I trust in Your promises, and I stand in expectation with hope for a pure heart and a renewed mind.
Romans 15:13 NIV

"Whoever believes in him is not condemned, but whoever does not believe stands condemned already because they have not believed in the name of God's one and only Son."

Father God, I am so glad that I believe in You, Your Son and in the Holy Ghost. Although I know trials and tribulations will come, I know without a doubt that my bad days will eventually turn into good days. Even when the enemy tries to still my joy by their cruel words, lack of transparency or deceit, I am more than a conqueror! I trust in Your promises, and I stand in expectation, drawing my circle to reap what You have already promised me.

John 3:18 NIV

~~~~~

"Many are the plans in a person's heart, but it is the Lord 's purpose that prevails."

Lord I pray daily for You to order my steps, and for You to guide me in the way I should go. Yes Lord, I am guilty at times for taking my life's decisions, desires and dreams into my own hands, and not allowing You to play a part. Please forgive me for not calling on You to guide my thinking so that the plans for me that You speak of in Jeremiah 29:11 actually are carried out according to Your Will and Your Way. Let Thy Will be done!

Proverbs 19:21 NIV

Grace and Mercy

I will be honest; I didn't really understand grace and mercy, and all that it meant in aligning my ways with God's ways. "Lord have mercy!" I can't think of the many times I used this request out of context, and in vain! Then my Bishop taught one Sunday on just what grace and mercy was and how it is manifested in our lives. This is what I came to understand: Mercy was not getting what you deserved; it is a withheld punishment. Grace was getting what you didn't deserve; an unmerited favor. Wow! What a revelation. With this new teaching, I went back and read about Job's time in the wilderness and his cry out to God. The following scripture made so much more sense. God provided Job with grace and mercy. Job 33:27,"I sinned and perverted what was right, but I did not get what I deserved. He redeemed my soul from going down to the pit, and I will live to enjoy the light of life." God does all these things to a man--twice, even three times--to turn back his soul from the pit that the light of life may shine on him."

God has provided me so much grace, especially when I think about some of life's woes that He did not allow me to experience. I am probably not supposed to be living right now, because I was in harm's way too many times to count. For the things He did allow me to experience, I am still grateful to Him for opening my eyes, which resulted in a testimony for so many others. God continues to send His angels to encamp around me, keeping me from harm's way.

I am so glad that I learned that God is a merciful God. It took me a minute to align my walk with His, and so, I can recall many times when I deserved to be punished. Covert manipulation, theft, exaggeration; I always found a way to get over! But thanks be to God, who was a forgiving God. He saw my ugly ways and transformed them into opportunities to help, guide, and provide comfort to others.

Remember, God has His hands on you. He says He will see you through, just hold your hands up high and give Him praise. How do you thank God for the grace and mercy he supplies in your life? Or do you take it for granted?

How do you thank God for His grace and mercy?

"Therefore, I urge you, brothers and sisters, in view of God's mercy, to offer your bodies as a living sacrifice, holy and pleasing to God—this is your true and proper worship."

Lord, help me to focus on my blessings. Help me to overcome negativity in my home, on my job, and among my peers. Make me confident so that I do not stoop down to evil. Keep me and deliver me from petty retaliation. Give me strength to do good in spite of what comes my way.

Romans 12:1 NIV

~~~~~

"Give praise to the Lord, proclaim his name; make known among the nations what he has done."

Thank you God for your grace and mercy. All that I have and all that I am, I owe it to you! I am not ashamed to speak about your goodness and love. Every chance I get, I will brag about the many times you have fought my battles by removing the thorns that try to steal my joy, take my peace, and contaminate my body. I am forever grateful!

1 Chronicles 16:8 NIV

~~~~~

"For the grace of God has appeared that offers salvation to all people."

Lord, thank you for your grace and your mercy! Without it I am not sure where I would be. Grace has allowed me to have many "do overs" and I am very grateful!

Titus 2:11 NIV

"Do not judge, and you will not be judged. Do not condemn, and you will not be condemned. Forgive, and you will be forgiven. Give, and it will be given to you. A good measure, pressed down, shaken together and running over, will be poured into your lap. For with the measure you use, it will be measured to you."

Lord, thank you for this reminder in your word for how I should treat others: family, friends, and strangers! Keep me from this vengeful thinking. Help me God to be free from behaving in such a manner, even if I have been offended in this way! Show me how to break this chain of thinking so that I can reap all the blessings that you have stored up for me. I thank you in advance for a pure mind and a pure heart, and for the strength to rise above immature thinking. Hallelujah!
Luke 6:37-38 NIV

"Come now, let us settle the matter," says the Lord. "Though your sins are like scarlet, they shall be as white as snow; though they are red as crimson, they shall be like wool."

Thank you Lord for transparency. For reminding me that my mistakes and poor decisions that cause unrest are forgiven by giving you reign over my life. Thank you for the deliverance from guilt.
Isaiah 1:18 NIV

"Know therefore that the Lord your God is God; he is the faithful God, keeping his covenant of love to a thousand generations of those who love him and keep his commandments."
Thank you God for your commitment to love me forever in spite of my wrongdoings, and for the strength to live in this world but not be of this world! Daily, I am consciously making sure that I follow your commandments so that it may be well with my mind, body, soul, job, health, and finances.
Deuteronomy 7:9 NIV

"Being confident of this, that he who began a good work in you will carry it on to completion until the day of Christ Jesus."
Thank you God for your commitment to my well-being. I know I can be hard-headed at times; wanting to do things my way! I am grateful for your time, patience, and love that allows me to get back on the right path towards salvation.
Let Thy Will be done!
Philippians 1:6 NIV

"For it is by grace you have been saved, through faith— and this is not from yourselves, it is the gift of God— not by works, so that no one can boast."
Thank you Lord for your grace and mercy. For always providing me a way out of my trials and tribulations. I am so glad that you have taught me how to rely on you in times of a health, financial, or relationship crisis. You are my rock and my redeemer! I owe everything I am to You.
Ephesians 2:8-9 NIV

"Whatever you have learned or received or heard from me, or seen in me—put it into practice. And the God of peace will be with you."
Thank you Lord for your great examples and modeling of perfection. I know that I am not perfect, but grateful that when you formed me in the womb, that it was after your own image. God, I thank you for your sound teaching; showing me how to give you my burdens, desires, and needs, and because of this I walk in peace daily.
Philippians 4:9 NIV

"Better is one day in your courts than a thousand elsewhere; I would rather be a doorkeeper in the house of my God than dwell in the tents of the wicked."
Thank you Lord for opening doors where bountiful blessings flow, and for giving me a discerning spirit that keeps me from those who bring chaos and strife.
Psalm 84:10 NIV

"I am the Alpha and the Omega," says the Lord God, "who is, and who was, and who is to come, the Almighty."
Lord, there is none like you. I will honor you presence at all times; when I am feeling happy, sad, sick, and sometimes confused. Thank you for your commitment to be available to heal, deliver, save and sanctify me throughout time. There are no substitutions for the type of relief you provide in joy and peace within me.
Revelations 1:8 NIV

"But he said to me, 'My grace is sufficient for you, for my power is made perfect in weakness.' Therefore I will boast all the more gladly about my weaknesses, so that Christ's power may rest on me."

Thank you God for your grace and mercy. I am not ashamed nor do I fear my weaknesses, because I know that your power will make me strong in time of need. Thank you in advance for strength when my heart, mind, and flesh become weak.

2 Corinthians 12:9 NIV

~~~~~

"For physical training is of some value, but godliness has value for all things, holding promise for both the present life and the life to come."

Lord, I thank you for the ability and energy to "work out" in an effort to keep my body physically strong and healthy. God, in the same way, build my stamina to read, learn, and meditate on your word. I know your word sustains all things and provides the strength that makes me strong during moments of weakness; heals my physical and emotional pain, keeping my mind clear of negative thoughts; and providing clarity and understanding to the chaos in my life. Thank you God for being my "work out" partner!

Timothy 4:8 NIV

Daily Spiritual Nugget

"so that with one mind and one voice you may glorify the God and Father of our Lord Jesus Christ."
With one mind, one voice, I will Honor you both with all my heart, with all that I am, and all that I strive to be; totally connected to Your Will and Your Way. Lord God I pray every day asking You to guide my walk and my talk. Thank you for the reminders in Your Word that provide me with strength and perseverance to stay in Your marvelous light. Some days are better than others, and so I am grateful for Your grace! Lord God, on my good days and through my storms, I will glorify You. I will speak of Your goodness, and I will shout aloud praises of Your mercy.
Romans 15:6 NIV

"The Lord is far from the wicked, but he hears the prayer of the righteous."
Lord, I pray daily that my words and actions are pleasing in your sight. I know that you know that I am not perfect, but yet you still honor my requests. Thank you for the correction that transforms my heart; creating a new thinking, a new language, and a new way to exist among others. Hallelujah!
Proverbs 15:29 NIV

"In your anger do not sin": Do not let the sun go down while you are still angry"

Oh Lord unharden my heart against those things and people who have caused my thoughts to be in conflict with Your ways. Oh Lord continue to create in me a pure heart. I thank You in advance for the spirit of forgiveness. I thank you Lord for showing me my heart daily so that I may not sin against You. Lord help me to let go of those things that I truly have no control of and to let You bear the burdens of worry, so that I do not worry in anger and resentment. Lord I thank You for thoughts of peace. I praise You for doing a good work in me so that my heart is satisfied with goodness and filled with love. When evil thoughts sneak in, help me to recognize my own wrong doing so that I can forgive immediately. I pray in advance for Your forgiveness and Your mercy Lord. Keep me evenly tempered in Your love and kindness.

Ephesians 4:26 NIV

~~~~~

"This is what the Lord says: "Restrain your voice from weeping and your eyes from tears, for your work will be rewarded," declares the Lord........"

Thank You Lord! Your Word also tells me to endure; joy does come in the morning. Give me strength to endure. So I will wait for my victory. I will wait for my deliverance. I will wait on Your perfect timing. It is comforting to know that my tears are not in vain. Thank You Lord for all of Your blessings.

Jeremiah 31:16 NIV

"But when you ask, you must believe and not doubt, because the one who doubts is like a wave of the sea, blown and tossed by the wind."

Thank You Lord God for this reminder in Your Word. ...to have faith as small as a mustard seed and KNOW that You keep Your promises. Honestly praying, this is sometimes difficult...to not doubt just a little. Especially when there are reoccurrences of similar situations. I know Lord that You have a plan for me as I journey along in this life, and my plan is to allow you to steer me in the right direction. So Lord I promise to work on being encouraged by the requests You have already blessed me with. I pray for daily strength to be grounded in Your Word, and to be able to stand strong during times of chaos, confusion and disappointments. Thank You Lord for Your protection and Your presence.

James 1:6 NIV

Constant Companion

When I think about what a constant companion is, and the characteristics that gives someone this honor, I think about the small circle of people in my life who have been "ride or die" friends who rode with me during emotional upsets, physical breakdowns, and financial losses. You never know who God will put in your path to bless you, help you, and to keep you from harm's way. God's Word says to treat others just like you would want to be treated at all times, and the blessings will be returned to you tenfold. God put men and women in my life who I could trust with my emotions, dark secrets, and desires that did not always align with God's way. I also realized that the key to knowing what God's plans were for me, I had to stay in close contact and build a relationship with Him. I didn't stop confiding in my friends, but I learned to confide in God first.

I thank God for all of His blessings. I thank God for guiding me in the right direction. I thank God for allowing me to live one day at a time, and I thank Him for His presence right on time. I thank God for His light that guides my walk each and every day; I thank God for the strength to kneel every morning to pray. I thank God for visions of things yet to come; I thank God for waking me every morning in my right mind and with wisdom. I thank God for the peace He gives in the midst of chaos; I thank God for the joy that comes in the morning and for giving me hope that my life is not lost.

I thank God for delivering me from myself, and embracing me in his arms to keep me protected in his love. Through daily prayer and worship, I opened my mind and heart to all of his wisdom and reaped blessings. When you call on Him, God will provide you an answer just for you in just the right time. In Matthew 16:15 God asked, "Who do you say I am?" It is unquestionable, He is my constant companion. He is my strength, my redeemer, my rock and my salvation. He is my friend and my lover. He is my healer and my Prince of Peace. He is my all in all. He is my first love. I will never forget about what He has done for me. He sacrificed His Son just for me! He is the Alpha and the Omega; no man has ever been greater. He is my joy, peace and happiness. He is my rock, and my strength comes from Him. He is my companion, and I put all of my trust In Him. He is a companion I will never depart from. Who is your constant companion? Do they accept you for who you are, and not for whom they want you to be?

Who is your constant companion, how do they treat you?

"I told you that you would die in your sins; if you do not believe that I am he, you will indeed die in your sins."
I know He lives in me, around me, and through me. I am because He says I am. I praise Him for living in me in spite of my filthy self. Amen.
John 8:24 NIV

~~~~~

"But what about you?" he asked. "Who do you say I am?"
He is my strength, my redeemer, my rock and my salvation. He is my friend and my lover. He is my healer and my Prince of Peace. He is my all in all. He is my first love.
Matthew 16:15 NIV

~~~~~

"Praise be to the God and Father of our Lord Jesus Christ, the Father of compassion and the God of all comfort."
Thank you Lord Jesus for sending the comforter to me so that I can remain faithful and trusting in you for all of my days. I will trust you until the day I die.
2 Corinthians 1:3 NIV

~~~~~

"Since you are my rock and my fortress, for the sake of your name lead and guide me."
Thank you for being my strong hold and giving the direction from which I travel. You are my rock and my strength. You provide the stability that allows my abilities to take charge and produce good works in your name sake. Lord you are my provider of all things. Amen.
Psalm 31:3 NIV

"For I am convinced that neither death nor life, neither angels nor demons, neither the present nor the future, nor any powers, neither height nor depth, nor anything else in all creation, will be able to separate us from the love of God that is in Christ Jesus our Lord."

Lord, my love is forever, and forever I pray I will be connected to you. You are in my thoughts when I rise and when I lay down. When chaos arises in my life, I will use that energy to strengthen and deepen my faith in you!

Romans 8:38-39 NIV

"Take my yoke upon you and learn from me, for I am gentle and humble in heart and you will find rest for your souls."

Thank you for finding the time to walk with me throughout my days. You are the perfect companion to spend my time with. Thank you for the guidance that allows me to keep moving forward. You have helped me and provided me the stamina to compete with the things of this world without me being stressed and overwhelmed. Without you I am nothing. I am alone. Thank you for holding my hand.

Matthew 11:29 NIV

"For I am not ashamed of the gospel, because it is the power of God that brings salvation to everyone who believes: first to the Jew, then to the Gentile."

Lord, you are my everything. There is none like you! I will speak of your goodness all the days of my life, even during times of pain and suffering. You are great!

Romans 1:16 NIV

Daily Spiritual Nugget

"Jesus looked at them and said, "With man this is impossible, but with God all things are possible."
Thank you Lord for making all things possible. I am forever indebted to you. You always make a way for me to see clearly through my storms. Even if it takes me time to see and hear you. You provide the answers. I rely on your guidance and wisdom to make all things new. Thank you for taking my pain away. Because of you, I am stronger, wiser, and confident that no weapon formed against me shall prosper!
Matthew 19:26 NIV

"If anyone acknowledges that Jesus is the Son of God, God lives in them and they in God."
I am so glad that I know you Lord and that you know my heart. Every day I strive to get intimately closer to you. Thank you for keeping your arms open to comfort me through my trials and tribulations, pain and sorrow. Thank you for being my healer and deliverer.
John 4:15 NIV

"However, I consider my life worth nothing to me; my only aim is to finish the race and complete the task the Lord Jesus has given me—the task of testifying to the good news of God's grace."
Lord, I am always careful to give your name praise every time I open my mouth, thanking you for the many blessings that you have provided, and for the peace that you provide during the chaos and crisis in my life. I know that without you I am nothing. With you I am everything.
Acts 20:24 NIV

"Praise be to the Lord, to God our Savior, who daily bears our burdens."
Praise ye the Lord! I thank you for being my stronghold, my rock and my deliverer. For the quiet peace that exists within me during the loud storms that sometimes come my way. Thank you for being my constant companion.
Psalm 68:19 NIV

"He who did not spare his own Son, but gave him up for us all—how will he not also, along with him, graciously give us all things?"
Thank you God for the ultimate sacrifice! Just for me, in spite of my many shortcomings, you continue to provide everything I need. The blessings are always on time indeed! The desires of my heart are comforted by your eternal love, and my mind rests in peace knowing how much you care. When others are not, you are always there!
Romans 8:32 NIV

"Give thanks to the Lord, for he is good; his love endures forever."
Lord, I am so thankful for your presence in my life. Through the good, you have been my joy and happiness. Through the pain, you have been my peace and love. On my worst days, you still come around to comfort me; providing me just what I need. I can always count on you when others have let me down. Thank you for being my friend, companion, and life coach.
Psalm 107:1 NIV

"And without faith it is impossible to please God, because anyone who comes to him must believe that he exists and that he rewards those who earnestly seek him."

Lord, I totally rely on Your presence in my life to guide me, provide for me, and deliver me from life's trials and tribulations. You are my constant companion that I trust with my whole heart forever. I will seek Your guidance before laboring within myself and among others. With You I am everything, without You I am nothing!

Hebrews 11:6 NIV

~~~~~

"Lord, you are my God; I will exalt you and praise your name, for in perfect faithfulness you have done wonderful things, things planned long ago."

Thank You Lord God for being attentive to my needs before I even know that I would have to call on You. You have been faithful in Your love and attention. I am so grateful that You accepted me with all my stuff. Thank You! I honor You, and praise Your Holy name. I glorify Your presence and will forever reverence your name

Isaiah 25:1 NIV

~~~~~

"if we are faithless, he remains faithful, for he cannot disown himself."

Thank you God for having faith in me during those times when I couldn't seem to see the light at the end of the tunnel. Your love provides me with hope when I am feeling hopeless. I am grateful for Your constant presence all around me, giving me direction to see clearly, think wisely, and walk upright. Father God, thank You for consistency when I am not. Thank you for just being God!

2 Timothy 2:13 NIV

"Therefore, there is now no condemnation for those who are in Christ Jesus, because through Christ Jesus the law of the Spirit who gives life has set you free from the law of sin and death."

Thank You Lord for setting me free from sin, and providing me an opportunity to live free! Lord I am grateful for Your Spirit of life that lives within me; releasing me from the bondage of sin behavior that keeps me sad, angry and depressed, Lord thank You for washing me clean from my mess. Lord thank You for life in the light! Thank You for Your covering that keeps me out of the darkness. Thank You for Your peace, Your grace and mercy, and above all, thank You for Your love. Continue to guide my walk so that I stay focused on You, I believe in Your Word and all that You promise to do.
Romans 8:1-2 NIV

~~~~~

"Know therefore that the Lord your God is God; he is the faithful God, keeping his covenant of love to a thousand generations of those who love him and keep his commandments."

Yes Lord God! I know that You exist, and that You are an awesome God! I know that You are real; I could be living a different life, and because of Your faithfulness to my war cry, I am who I am today. Thank You for Your presence around my good and not so good moments. Thank you for saving me! Thank you for sending the Holy Spirit to comfort me when my faith becomes faint and my mind wanders away from Your commands. Lord God I love You, and I am so grateful that You love me too! Hallelujah!
Deuteronomy 7:9 NIV

"Lord , you are the God who saves me; day and night I cry out to you."

Thank you Lord God for hearing my prayers and making Your presence known. When others let me down, Your timing is always right on time. When I let my own self down; falling weak to the ways of this world, You are still there to remind me that You got my back! Hallelujah! I pray daily for You to keep my ears clear of the white noise, so that I can hear Your voice clearly when You speak. Thank you God for Your patience, love, and Your Grace that keeps me from harm's way from day to day.

Psalm 88:1 NIV

Strength

When we think about strength and where it comes from, we often first think about the physical strength that we have from working out in the gym, or the daily exercise regimen we put our bodies through to stay strong. Webster describes strength as the quality or state of being strong; the power to resist strain or stress, durability. But what does it mean to have strength in the Lord? I quickly figured that out during and after my divorce. To say I was feeling weak would be an understatement. In His Word, God promised to provide me with all of my needs and desires (Deuteronomy 30:16, NIV). I submitted to God and allowed him to fight my battles in and out of the courtroom; I turned all of my sorrows over to God, and let the One who has always had my back handle it!

"Blessed is the one who perseveres under trial because, having stood the test, that person will receive the crown of life that the Lord has promised to those who love him." (James 1:12 NIV). His Word told me to be strong in Him, rely on Him, and He would give me the strength I needed to get through my pain. And as promised, He did! He gave me the courage to step out on faith to deal with some of life's challenges, and the strength to persevere through the storms that tried to keep me from achieving success. I know it was because I put my full trust in Him and not in man, that I have been able to press my way through. He protected me when I was being attacked. His Word provided just what I needed; wisdom to think positive and to stand strong in expectation with hope, and in peace. In return, I try my best to live according to His Word daily. When I began to live as God instructed, He built my strength and endurance, and many unexpected blessings came my way. No machine or exercise can compare to the strength that God gives us when we let Him handle our battles.

Not only did my strength keep me walking, but it kept me walking with my head held high, finally proud of who I was and who I had become in God. This strength provided me with an eternal peace that provided a covering for any future pain or disappointment. My strength allowed me to forge ahead seeking the best in all I do. God's strength gave me hope, made me courageous, and intensified my faith. No weapon formed against me shall prosper! How strong are you? Where does your strength come from?

Where does your strength come from?

"So I was left alone, gazing at this great vision; I had no strength left, my face turned deathly pale and I was helpless."
Lord, give me the strength to sustain and maintain a commitment to you. Provide me a word each day that will allow me to be encouraged and to encourage others. Open my eyes, mind, and ears to hear, meditate, and hear from you, while also discerning those things that are not good for those in the world.
Daniel 10:8 NIV

~~~~~

"You, my brothers and sisters, were called to be free. But do not use your freedom to indulge the flesh; rather, serve one another humbly in love."
Lord, thank you for providing me with strength to break the chains of adversity in my life daily. Keep me from being selfish. Show me how to use the gifts from you to help my family, friends, and my enemies.
Galatians 5:13 NIV

~~~~~

"Those who cling to worthless idols turn away from God's love for them."
Wow! God I don't ever want to lose your love! Give me strength to let go of those things, behaviors, and people who cause me to sometimes take my focus from you. Lord, show me how to balance my time, and to keep my mind renewed. I pray that everything I do is done in decency and order. I will diligently give you glory in all that I do!
Jonah 2:8 NIV

"Even youths grow tired and weary, and young men stumble and fall; but those who hope in the Lord will renew their strength. They will soar on wings like eagles; they will run and not grow weary, they will walk and not be faint."

Lord, I am so glad that I believe in you and you believe in me. I know you are my rock and my strength. My deliverer from chaos and confusion. Thank you Lord for renewing me daily.

Isaiah 40:30-31 NIV

"The Sovereign lord is my strength; he makes my feet like the feet of a deer, he enables me to tread on the heights. For the director of music. On my stringed instruments."

Thank you Lord for giving me the tools to withstand those things that are hard and difficult. Thank you for directing my path so that my situations result in peace, and are filled with joy.

Habakkuk 3:19 NIV

"For we are God's handiwork, created in Christ Jesus to do good works, which God prepared in advance for us to do."

Thank you God for the good in me. Thank you for creating in me a pure heart filled with love; that in spite of trials and tribulations, I still have peace and joy. Jesus, continue to dwell your spirit in me, so that my talk and my walk are aligned with your ways. Keep my thoughts from thinking evil when life's woes come my way. Instead, help me to find the strength to pray.

Ephesians 2:10 NIV

"The grass withers and the flowers fall, but the word of our God endures forever."

Lord, I am so glad that Your presence can withstand the elements that change the seasons. Like glue, Your Word seals and mends broken hearts; making the mind and body feel revived and like new. Thank you for being my stronghold and my constant companion.

Isaiah 40:8 NIV

"Be strong and very courageous. Be careful to obey all the law my servant Moses gave you; do not turn from it to the right or to the left, that you may be successful wherever you go."

Lord, help me to be strong in Your Word so that my actions demonstrate courageous behaviors. Thank you for Your guidance and strength. I pray that it allows me to do a good work at home, in the community, on the job, and among family and friends. Lord, use me for Your glory!

Joshua 1:7 NIV

"Since you are my rock and my fortress, for the sake of your name lead and guide me."

Thank you for being my strong hold; providing me with Your sword as my weapon against evil-doers, evil people and evil things of this world. You are my rock and my strength. You make me feel strong when I am weak and happy when I am sad. I pray that my abilities take charge and produce good works in Your name sake! Lord, you are my provider of all things. Amen.

Psalm 31:3 NIV

"Brothers and sisters, I do not consider myself yet to have taken hold of it. But one thing I do: Forgetting what is behind and straining toward what is ahead, I press on toward the goal to win the prize for which God has called me heavenward in Christ Jesus."

Lord, I continue to be a work in progress especially as I work through past hurts, loss of loved ones, disappointments, pain and rejection. I will only think on those things as testimonies; sharing with others how You blessed me and delivered me from them all! Thank you for the strength and determination to live free from bondage so that I can focus on the blessings yet to come. Hallelujah!

Philippians 3:13-14 NIV

~~~~~

"Forget the former things, do not dwell on the past."

Lord, thank you for another year, another opportunity to get it right, and more time to live my life in Your marvelous light. I am keeping my eyes on the prize and moving forward. Thank you for keeping my mind focused on the blessings to come, and not the pain and disappointments from my yesterdays. I stand in expectation for You to make all things new, praying and fasting just to get closer to You.

Isaiah 43:18 NIV

"There is no one holy like the Lord; there is no one besides you; there is no Rock like our God."
Lord God You are the one true God and there is none like You. There is not one man that can do what You do! You give life to the lifeless, strength to the weak, and joy to the unhappy. I thank You Lord for Your unconditional love. Unlike man, You keep no records of my wrongdoing, and I am grateful that each day You allow me to have, I am able to start over again. Thank You Lord God for Your Grace and Mercy.
1 Samuel 2:2 NIV

"Look to the Lord and his strength; seek his face always."
Lord in everything I do, I try to remember to seek You first to provide the direction in which I should go. I look to You for the wisdom to weigh the good and the bad before I react. I look for Your protection against the evil that might be lurking about waiting for me to fail. I look for You to comfort me when I feel alone. I look to You for peace when people around me appear to be in chaos. Lord I look to You to provide me the strength to overcome my weaknesses that prevent me from living a prosperous life. Lord thank You for making it easy to seek You through prayer, fasting and reading Your Word.
1 Chronicles 16:11 NIV

"Restore to me the joy of your salvation and grant me a willing spirit, to sustain me."

Father I come to You in prayer as humble as I know how, asking for forgiveness of any negative actions or reactions towards others that were not pleasing in Your sight. Father God I thank You in advance for Your strength to overcome weaknesses that cause me to fall. Lord restore in me a spirit of forgiveness, love, joy, peace and thanksgiving.
Psalm 51:12 NIV

"And the God of all grace, who called you to his eternal glory in Christ, after you have suffered a little while, will himself restore you and make you strong, firm and steadfast."

Lord I pray for joy and peace as I go through my wilderness experiences. I thank You God in advance for restoration; an opportunity to be transformed in my thinking, and in my actions, and all for Your glory. I thank You for the strength to persevere through adversity; praying faithfully, and standing firm on Your promises to make all things new. I shall wait on You Lord God...have Your Way!
1 Peter 5:10 NIV

"In him and through faith in him we may approach God with freedom and confidence."

Thank You Lord Jesus for bearing my burdens so that I may reverence the Father with a faith that is beyond measure. Because of Your suffering, I can walk upright without shame of wrongdoing. Thank You for providing me with the confidence to come to the Father with hope, and expectancy to receive an infinity of blessings. Because of You, I am stronger and wiser. I rejoice in the midst of uncertainty, because I trust with an open heart filled with love and thanksgiving. Thank You Father God for allowing me to be in Your presence.

Ephesians 3:12 NIV

"Turn my eyes away from worthless things; preserve my life according to your word."

Yes Lord! Help me to not waste my time on the things in this life that are useless, senseless, and definitely worthless! I pray that every day is a day full of meaning and purpose. Let Your light shine within me so that every situation I engage in, and every person I encounter, my actions and reactions reflect Your purpose for me on this earth. I pray that my time and talk are not wasted on useless chatter that does not build or extend Your kingdom. I pray that every day is a day that I am glorifying You with words, actions and in deeds.

Psalm 119:37 NIV

Protection

How do you protect yourself, your feelings, your emotions, and your body from people who seek to harm you? Do you fight back, or do you just give in? Well, I did a little of both. Fighting back was my way of denying what was really happening to me. Doing nothing was me just tired of fighting! I eventually asked God to join this war. First, I asked Him to hold my tongue to keep me from engaging in any unnecessary agitation. Secondly, I asked Him to show me a way out of this unhealthy relationship. Lastly, I asked Him to open my eyes to see what life God really wanted for me. This is when I began practicing my new understanding of faith. I began to pray and leave my sorrows with God. It was hard not to take things back, but God showed me over and over, that He had my back.

As I communed in prayer with God, He led me to two scriptures. These scriptures became my daily mantra that I began to recite when I awoke and before I closed my eyes at night:

- *"But the Lord is faithful. He will establish you and guard you against the evil one." (2 Thessalonians 3:3)*

- *"The Lord is my rock, my fortress and my deliverer, my God is my rock, in whom I take refuge, my shield and the horn of my salvation. He is my stronghold, my refuge and my savior from violent people you save me." (2 Samuel 22:3-4)*

With prayer, fasting and reciting the Word, I was able to let go and let God protect me in my home, on the job, with family, and from all evil that tried to come my way. I thanked God daily for His peace in the midst of my storms, and His strength to still praise Him in song. I prayed daily for God's Spirit to reside in me; to have reign over me on my sunny days, as well as on my rainy days. Over and over, I asked God to consume my mind, body and soul, to keep me focused in all of His righteous ways.

I learned to laugh in the midst of my storm. To laugh even louder in the great depths of my pain. I smiled often to keep my face from wrinkling in depression. I kept a pep in my step to stay ahead of the blessings that I knew My God had promised me. I walked humbly allowing God to guide every step. I kept my mind engaged in service to others, while bonding in sisterhood with my Sorors, and creating hope in the lives of children in the public school system. Psalm 27 also reminded me about God's protection. Specifically in verse 5: "...For in the day of trouble he will keep me safe in his dwelling; he will hide me in the shelter of his sacred tent and set me high upon a rock." Through prayer, praise and meditation, I sought the Lord's presence and protection. I thank Him every day for providing rest and refuge. I survived, and it was because of God's protection. Who is your protector?

How do you protect yourself from evil?

"Look to the Lord and his strength; seek his face always."
Lord, I look to You daily; seeking your face for wisdom, understanding, and guidance through life's challenges. I wear Your shield of faith to keep me guarded from evil, and I carry Your sword in my heart so that Your spirit will reside in me. Thank you for equipping me with the strength and courage that allows me to stand tall in the face of any trial.
Psalm 105:4 NIV

"So do not fear, for I am with you; do not be dismayed, for I am your God. I will strengthen you and help you; I will uphold you with my righteous right hand."
Lord, please keep Your hand on me to keep me from all of my ways. Your love and kindness is just what I need as I try to begin every day better than the day before. I am so grateful for your love that protects me through my good, as well as my bad days. Thank you God for bearing my burdens! For picking me up when I fall to sin, for giving me hope when I feel hopeless, and strength when I feel weakened in my mind and slowful in my body. You are my DELIVERER!
Isaiah 41:10 NIV

"You are the light of the world. A town built on a hill cannot be hidden."
Thank you God for shining Your bright light over my life. Your light provides me direction on what to say and do. It helps to keep me out of dark places. It protects, it heals, and it sanctifies. Thank you!
Matthew 5:4 NIV

Daily Spiritual Nugget

"For it is God's will that by doing good you should silence the ignorant talk of foolish people. Live as free people, but do not use your freedom as a cover-up for evil; live as God's slaves."

Wow God! Thank you for your spirit that lives within me. It often keeps me from evil and from speaking lies. I am grateful for the light that shines within, it reflects bright for others to see; it allows me to discern the evil ways of others. Hallelujah!

1 Peter 2:15-16 NIV

"I am the lord, and there is no other; apart from me there is no God. I will strengthen you, though you have not acknowledged me, so that from the rising of the sun to the place of its setting people may know there is none besides me. I am the lord, and there is no other."

Thank you God for always reminding me that you are always around, keeping me, holding me, and supporting me. Thanks for having my back through all of my circumstances! Even when I don't call on you for help you still surround me with your wisdom and love.

Isaiah 45:5 NIV

"No, in all these things we are more than conquerors through him who loved us."

Thank you Lord for having my back. I know that as long as I trust in you I can do anything!

Romans 8:37 NIV

"Trust in the lord with all your heart and lean not on your own understanding; in all your ways submit to him, and he will make your paths straight."
Thank you God for instilling in me the confidence that allows me to put my trust in you and you only. Thanks in advance for allowing me to give my concerns to you while you mend my heart from the trials I go through. Thank you in advance for my healing from sickness, for increasing my finances, and for taking care of my family and friends far and near.
Proverbs 3:4 NIV

"Better is one day in your courts than a thousand elsewhere; I would rather be a doorkeeper in the house of my God than dwell in the tents of the wicked."
Thank you Lord for opening doors where bountiful blessings flow and for giving me a discerning spirit that keeps me from those who bring chaos and strife.
Psalm 84:10 NIV

"So do not fear, for I am with you; do not be dismayed, for I am your God. I will strengthen you and help you; I will uphold you with my righteous right hand."
Thank you God for standing with me in times of trouble. For healing the sickness in my body and in my mind. I am so glad that I can count on you when others turn their backs. I am forever grateful to you for turning my sorrows into joy and my chaos into peace. I love you Lord!
Isaiah 41:10 NIV

"He who earnestly seeks after and craves righteousness, mercy, and loving-kindness will find life in addition to righteousness (uprightness and right standing with God) and honor."
Thank you God for the energy and the desire to seek good things that honor you in my sometimes chaotic life.
Proverbs 21:21 AMP

"In addition to all this, take up the shield of faith, with which you can extinguish all the flaming arrows of the evil one."
Lord, thank you for Your mighty hand of power that provides a way out of no way. I thank you for the strong covering which protects me from myself, others, and the evil things of this world. Thank you for providing clarity in my mind so that I have a steadfast focus on just what I need to do when chaos and evil come my way; experiencing a sound mind of peace in the midst of the storms! Hallelujah!
Ephesians 6:16 NIV

"Do not be anxious about anything, but in every situation, by prayer and petition, with thanksgiving, present your requests to God."
Lord, I thank you for showing me how to change my worry list into a prayer list. I thank you for listening to my requests for a pure heart, a sound mind, and a healthy body. I am not just informing You, but I want to invite You into my heart and soul. Thank you in advance for the intimacy, direction, and release from life's burdens! Hallelujah!
Philippians 4:6 NIV

"Do not say, "I'll pay you back for this wrong!" Wait for the Lord, and he will avenge you."
Thank You Lord for Your protection. I am so grateful that I can count on You to resolve my issues and concerns that I have with others. Show me how to wait on You for all things. I pray for an abundance of patience as I pray circles around increased finances, a healthy body free from pain and disease, and wisdom to make the right decisions about life, love and relationships. Lord thank You for always having my back!
Proverbs 20:22 NIV

~~~~~

"When I am afraid, I put my trust in you."
Thank You Lord for being so trustworthy. You never let me down; I can always count on You to be around. There are times when I let my fears consume my thoughts and I have to remind myself what Your Word says.... trust in You and NOT lean on my own understanding. So Lord give me strength to pray intentionally; praying circles around all of my hopes and dreams, and trusting in You to help me see my dreams come true. Lord I put my trust in You to heal my body from sickness. I trust You with managing my finances. I trust You to restore family and friend relationships. I trust You to bring peace and professionalism in the work place. I trust You to deliver me from those things that don't please You. Lord I trust in Your love, protection and all that You promise in Your Word that You say You will do.
Psalm 56:3 NIV

Daily Spiritual Nugget

"Humility is the fear of the Lord; its wages are riches and honor and life."

Father God I seek You in prayer daily with a humbled heart, asking You to guide where I walk, how I walk, how I talk and what I say. I pray for Your guidance on living according to Your Will and Your Way. Your Word teaches me to humble myself under Your mighty hand and power, and I will be exalted at Your designated time....Lord I am patiently waiting! I trust in Your teaching and I believe that You can provide all that I need.....help me to stay out of Your way Lord. I honor You for Your excellence, I commend You for Your faithfulness and love.... Lord God You are worthy to be praised.

Proverbs 22:4 NIV

"Our God is a God who saves; from the Sovereign Lord comes escape from death."

Thank You God for Your promise to provide protection against the evil things in this world. I know I have to do my part by following Your precepts, and aligning my ways with Your Word. Daily I seek Your face in prayer, asking for Your forgiveness of any sinful acts; known and unknown, so that I may exist in Your marvelous light. Save me oh Lord!

Psalm 68:20 NIV

Daily Spiritual Nugget

"You are my refuge and my shield; I have put my hope in your word."
Oh God, You are my refuge, shield, deliverer, comforter; You are my all in all. I put my hope and trust in You for all the days of my life. When man lets me down, I know that You are always there to pick me back up. Thank You for Your love and protection against the evil in this world. Thank You for Your guidance through troubled times and chaotic moments. Thank You for delivering me from my wretched self, others, and from those things that kept me out of Your Will. Your Word feeds my heart and mind with praise, thanksgiving, peace and joy. Because of Your love I feel whole
Psalm119:114 NIV

"Those who trust in the Lord are like Mount Zion, which cannot be shaken but endures forever."
Oh Lord, I trust You with all of my heart, my mind and my soul. You are my strength, and so everything I am, and everything I have is because of You. You are my peace in the midst of the raging storms that occur at home, on the job, and with family and friends. You are my joy during times of sadness and defeat. You are my deliverer who has rescued me from those habits and those people, that kept me bound in a state of complacency, depression, and doubt. So Lord for as long as I have breath in this life, I will praise You, honor Your presence, and have faith in Your promises.
Psalm 125:1 NIV

Daily Spiritual Nugget

Reflection and Practice

Name three steps you can take to get closer to God:

1.

2.

3.

Name three ways to find joy in the midst of your chaos:

1.

2.

3.

Name three other people who you can pray with:

1.

2.

3.

Name three things you are willing to give up to live according to God's Will and His Way:

1.

2.

3.

Identify three ways you can show God that you love him:

1.

2.

3.

Identify three weaknesses. What can you do to build your strength?

1.

2.

3.

Name three *Fruits of the Spirit* and identify how you will demonstrate them to others:

1.

2.

3.

Identify three ways to protect yourself from the enemy:

1.

2.

3.

Additional Prayers for Healing

Trust In His Word

"For if you forgive other people when they sin against you, your heavenly Father will also forgive you. But if you do not forgive others their sins, your Father will not forgive your sins."
Father God continue to renew my mind and restore my heart from anger, hurt and disappointment felt because I allowed others to offend me. Purify my heart and mind with clean thoughts full of love, peace and forgiveness.
Matthew 6:14-15 NIV

~~~~~

"And God is able to bless you abundantly, so that in all things at all times, having all that you need, you will abound in every good work."
Thank You God! Thank You for the opportunity to receive from You an abundance of love and protection for all that I am, all that I do, and everywhere that I want to go. I pray for an abundance of strength to be able to carry all that You give. I pray for an abundance of sight to be able to see clearly all that You have for me to see. Lord, I pray for a solid ground to walk on so that while I journey through this life, I walk In confidence, with wisdom and on peace.
Thank You for making all things new!
2 Corinthians 9:8 NIV

"If we live, we live for the Lord; and if we die, we die for the Lord. So, whether we live or die, we belong to the Lord."

Father God thank you for this confirmation in Your Word...life or death, we belong to You! No matter what the circumstances that bring death to our doorstep, the comfort and peace that we have, is knowing that we are children of the most High God. Help us Lord to have understanding! Thank You God for Your presence here on earth to provide comfort during times of adversity; we are not alone and we do not have to mourn alone....we have You to call on for strength. Thank you!

Romans 14:8 NIV

~~~~~

"Look to the Lord and his strength; seek his face always."

Lord I have my eyes on You, praying and fasting for my ways to be just like You. I look to You when life is good, and when tribulations arise, I put my trust in You to dry the tears in my eyes. Thank you for the strength that allows me to stand strong, I am grateful for Your presence which helps me daily to sing a new song. I look to You to make all things new, I am do thankful that You abide in me and I abide in You.

Psalm 105:4 NIV

"And this is love: that we walk in obedience to his commands. As you have heard from the beginning, his command is that you walk in love."

Thank You God for this reminder in Your Word. I know the command to love is more than just a rule to follow, but it is the action that represents who You are. We must love because You love unconditionally. So Lord God continue to purify my heart. Show me how to truly love those who have caused harm/death; those who offend by their words and actions; those who lack the ability to show compassion and those who lack love themselves.

2 John 1:6 NIV

~~~~~

"if my people, who are called by my name, will humble themselves and pray and seek my face and turn from their wicked ways, then I will hear from heaven, and I will forgive their sin and will heal their land."

Lord God I come to You daily, humbled in my thoughts, praying faithfully to seek Your face so that I can hear from You and feel Your presence. Lord God, I ask for forgiveness from known and unknown sin, and pray that my ways are pleasing to Your sight. When they are not, I will humbly receive the Holy Spirit's conviction and do my best to turn from my wicked ways. Lord God I pray that You will hear my voice through praise and supplication; honoring my requests for forgiveness, peace, joy and happiness. Thank You Lord God for love and kindness.

2 Chronicles 7:14 NIV

"And we know that in all things God works for the good of those who love him, who have been called according to his purpose."

In all things......health, finances, family, friends, work and relationships; Lord I pray that wherever You see wrong that You would help me to make it right so that I am living according to Your Will and Your Way. In all things, I put my trust in You to make all things new. Thank You God for putting Your trust in me!

Romans 8:28 NIV

"Accept one another, then, just as Christ accepted you, in order to bring praise to God."

Lord Jesus I want to live just like You! I want to be able to love unconditionally, trust without fear, and have the faith as small as a mustard seed. I pray that I can show all these things with and to all people, especially those who live in the dark. Those who have offended, mistreated, manipulated, took me for granted, and hurt me. I want to honor the presence of God that I know resides in me, so help me Lord! Continue to abide in me. Purify my thoughts. Clean my heart of animosity and judgment. Keep my tongue sweet so that out of my mouth words speak in love; with compassion, admiration and thanksgiving. Lord have Your Way. Lord I thank You for Your power to make all things new. I thank You for a new mind, a new heart, a new peace and a new joy! I pray that family and friends who struggle with unforgiveness, that they would seek Your presence and align their ways with Your Way.

Romans 15:7 NIV

"**Command those who are rich in this present world not to be arrogant nor to put their hope in wealth, which is so uncertain, but to put their hope in God, who richly provides us with everything for our enjoyment."**
Lord I will put my faith, trust and hope in You for the rest of my life. Thank You Lord, for everything I have and everything I am, is because of You. You always know just what to do! No money or anything else can take the place or have Your kind of results. Lord please forgive me if I have held people, places or other things in higher esteem than You. Only You can help make my hopes and dreams come true.
1 Timothy 6:17 NIV

Wait on the Lord

"He says, "Be still, and know that I am God; I will be exalted among the nations, I will be exalted in the earth."
Thank You Lord God once again for stepping in and having my back. I know who You are, and I believe in what You can do. There are times when I want quick results for the issues that sometimes create obstacles in my daily walk, and I want a resolution as quick as an eye blinks! So I pray for an abundance of patience and wisdom to call on You first, and then to wait on Your presence. Lord I ask that You take out the senseless noise in my ears so I can hear You clearly. Give me strength so that my faith in Your promises does not waver. Give me peace in my heart about the decisions and choices that have to be made, and show me how to let go of those things that I can't control.
Psalm 46:10 NIV

"Wait for the Lord ; be strong and take heart and wait for the Lord."

Oh Lord, I know that my requests don't always get an immediate response, and that You respond when it is the right time for me to receive. I pray for strength to overcome my desire of wanting to do things in my own way. Please bless me with an abundance of patience, so that I do not interfere with what You have planned for me. I give You glory, and honor You for all that You have already given me. Thank You God for talking charge over my life.

Psalm 27:14 NIV

~~~~~

"So do not throw away your confidence; it will be richly rewarded."

Thank You God for reminding me in Your Word to not give up, but instead to persevere! Sometimes it seems easier to drop doing or push through life's daily challenges, because we don't want to feel the pain that often comes with disappointment. Sometimes we even allow others to make us believe that what we have to contribute, what we have to say does not matter. But thanks be to You God for Your unwavering hope, trust and belief. I pray for pure confidence, not arrogance, not selfishness, and Lord please don't let my confidence be perceived as boasting.

Hebrews 10:35 NIV

"You need to persevere so that when you have done the will of God, you will receive what he has promised."
Oh Lord I pray for an abundance of strength as I go through my good days and my bad days. Help me to maneuver through the obstacles that sometimes get in my way of progressing forward. Show me through Your Word how to deal with life's challenges that become barriers. Oh Lord I thank You for Your presence and guidance. Daily I read, pray, and meditate on Your Word so that my ways become Your ways. Lord I pray that I am living a life that is pleasing to You. I am hopeful and faithfully committed to wait on Your promises and all that You say You will do.
Hebrews 10:36 NIV

"But godliness with contentment is great gain."
Lord God thank You for this reminder in Your Word. ...to be satisfied with who I am and what I have. Your Word says to not worry about the things of this world....so Lord I put my trust in You, trying my best to wait patiently on Your promises. I know You already know what I stand in need of Lord, so I am seeking You and all of Your righteousness! I know I can do and have everything I need through You who gives me strength. I am casting all my cares on You Lord, so I pray NOT for a covetous spirit, but a spirit of thanksgiving with satisfaction and peace on my mind and in my heart. Thank You for supplying all of my needs and not my wants. I have faith and know that You will cause all things to work for my good!
1 Timothy 6:6 NIV

"Bless those who curse you, pray for those who mistreat you."

Wow Lord, this is asking a lot! However Lord, thank You for this reminder in Your Word....treat people with love and respect, even though they treat you with hate and malice! Sometimes this is a difficult task, especially when my feelings have been hurt and I have been offended. I know Your Word says vengeance is Yours.....so Lord give me strength during those moments! Keep my tongue from speaking harm, and my mind from thinking evil. Let Your light shine through me so that evil cowers and moves away. Use me as a vessel to permeate good thoughts and feelings among others. Thoughts of love, peace, joy and happiness.
Luke 6:28 NIV

"If anyone turns a deaf ear to my instruction, even their prayers are detestable."

Lord Your Word says lean not to my own understanding.... And so Lord I try my very best to turn to You when I need to decide what to do when confronted with some of life's challenges. Honestly praying, sometimes it is difficult to wait to hear a word from You Lord, my patience runs out and I want what I want in that moment. Please forgive me Lord. I know Your timing is right on time, and You bless when I am not thinking and acting with a reprobate mind. So Lord give me strength to deny myself in those moments when I am feeling anxious to get things done my way. Give me an abundance of patience so that my actions are a reflection of Your direction. Hear my prayer oh Lord!
Proverbs 28:9 NIV

"If we endure, we will also reign with him. If we disown him, he will also disown us;

Lord please continue to show me in Your Word how to stand strong against others and those things that are of and represent evil. I pray for a spirit of discernment to provide me the wisdom to know when to walk away and when to keep my mouth closed. Daily I strive to be a good representation of You; loving, giving, caring, and at peace. Thank You Lord for keeping Your light shining on me and providing me Your grace and mercy. God I am thanking You in advance for the endurance to pray circles continuously around my needs, and the patience to wait on You to fulfill my requests.

2 Timothy 2:12 NIV

~~~~~

"Look to the Lord and his strength; seek his face always."

Lord in everything I do, I try to remember to seek You first to provide the direction in which I should go. I look to You for the wisdom to weigh the good and the bad before I react. I look for Your protection against the evil that might be lurking about waiting for me to fail. I look for You to comfort me when I feel alone. I look to You for peace when people around me appear to be in chaos. Lord I look to You to provide me the strength to overcome my weaknesses that prevent me from living a prosperous life. Lord thank You for making it easy to seek You through prayer, fasting and reading Your Word.

1 Chronicles 16:11 NIV

"Do not be quickly provoked in your spirit, for anger resides in the lap of fools."

Oh Lord! I am praying honestly, there are people; things that they say, how they act, and things that they do, that make it very difficult to not become angry. Help me Lord! Continue to hear my prayers requesting for you to hold my tongue, so that my words do not spew words that are not pleasing to Your ears. Give me clarity to the reasons why my anger exists. Purify my heart of any animosity towards that person, place or thing that fuels the negative energy in my body, so that my heart speaks good thoughts to my mind.

Ecclesiastes 7:9 NIV

"It is for freedom that Christ has set us free. Stand firm, then, and do not let yourselves be burdened again by a yoke of slavery."

Thank You Lord for the opportunity to live free. Thank you in advance for the coverage to speak up and not be bound to the vindictive and evil ways of others. I pray for a clear voice to speak what needs to be spoken without anger and without being too passive. I put on the shield of faith, and stand still so I can remain in Your Will, and You can have Your Way.

Galatians 5:1 NIV

"Through Jesus, therefore, let us continually offer to God a sacrifice of praise—the fruit of lips that openly profess his name."

Forever and ever Lord, I will praise You, especially when I encounter obstacles, I will praise You for the strength to get me through. I will wait patiently on the lesson to be learned and then stand in expectation for the blessing to come. I will praise Your name and give You glory a loud and in my secret place.

Hebrews 13:15 NIV

"Let perseverance finish its work so that you may be mature and complete, not lacking anything."

Thank You Lord God for the strength to keep pushing forward through my trials and tribulations. This journey through life has provided good and bad moments, and I am so grateful and thankful that I know You! I am so glad that You are a forgiving God that loves unconditionally. Even in my storms, complaining about my circumstance, You provide a sense of peace, understanding and a praise of thanksgiving. Thank You Lord God for sharing Your light which often guides me through adversity; providing me with clarity, so that I understand the power in You. You have the power to make all things new! So Lord God, I will press on, forgetting about all those trying moments from the past, and focusing forward to a prosperous life filled with joy, hope, love, peace and happiness.

James 1:4 NIV

"Those who guard their lips preserve their lives, but those who speak rashly will come to ruin."
Lord God I pray, let the words of my mouth be the meditation of my heart! Lord purify my heart, cleanse it from all evil thinking, so that my thoughts form words that speak praise, thanksgiving, joy and peace. Even when others speak on things that are not pleasing to me, I pray Lord that You will help me form words that are pleasing to You.
Proverbs 13:3 NIV

~~~~~

"But if we hope for what we do not yet have, we wait for it patiently."
Yes Lord! Although it is difficult to do at times, I understand Lord God why waiting is necessary. My life is not my own, my heart and my mind belong to You! When I wait on You, You bless beyond what I am hoping to come true. When I wait on You praying and fasting, I spend more time getting closer to You. When I wait on You, You guide me through unforeseen obstacles, giving me the strength to make it through. When I wait on You, what I hope for arrives right on time, not before I have a chance to purify my heart and mind. I know You want to make sure that I am ready to receive, so that You get the glory and it's all about You. I pray for strength and an abundance of patience to wait on You for every desire and wish I want to come true.
Romans 8:25 NIV

> "Every good and perfect gift is from above, coming down from the Father of the heavenly lights, who does not change like shifting shadows."

Thank You God for the many gifts that I have been blessed to receive; Gifts of hearing, speaking, giving and receiving. Thank You for their timely presence in my life as I grow spiritually; using them for good and not of evil. I pray that wisdom shows me when, how, and with whom to activate these gifts; sharing with compassion in love and thanksgiving. I pray that family and friends also recognize their gifts, using them in love to create joy and peace.
James 1:17 NIV

God loves you

> "Search me, God, and know my heart; test me and know my anxious thoughts. See if there is any offensive way in me, and lead me in the way everlasting"

Oh Lord, I pray that You continue to purify my heart, my mind and my thoughts that become words, so that my ways align with Your Will and Your Way. So show me Lord my faults, my imperfections, and those habits that keep me out of Your Will. I pray for forgiveness for known and unknown weaknesses that are disobedient to Your Way. Thank You for Your Grace and Your Mercy, and Your everlasting love that keeps me!
Psalm 139:23-24 NIV

"Cast your cares on the Lord and he will sustain you; he will never let the righteous be shaken."

Thank You Lord God for allowing me to bring you all of my pains, stresses, anxieties, and burdens. Thank You Lord, through Your Word, I am able to find the strength to go through life's challenges knowing that You have my back. It is Your Word where I find comfort when the enemy tries to attack. Even when it appears that all is lost, Your Word reminds me to have hope, because of Your son Jesus's death on the cross. Thank You God for Your promise to protect, provide peace and everlasting love.

Psalm 55:22 NIV

~~~~~

"If anyone destroys God's temple, God will destroy that person; for God's temple is sacred, and you together are that temple."

Thank You God for Your presence and Your protection. I am of importance! Continue to show me the fruits of Your goodness. I know that what I eat, how I exercise, and how I use my body, keeps it free from sickness and abuse. Oh Lord I pray for a temple that is healthy, wise, full of love, integrity, passion and thanksgiving. Help me to be conscientious about what goes in and how it comes out.......praying that my output aligns with your Word and Your Way.

1 Corinthians 3:17 NIV

"Nothing in all creation is hidden from God's sight. Everything is uncovered and laid bare before the eyes of him to whom we must give account."

Lord I know everything that is done in the dark, eventually comes to the light. So Lord I pray that all I do and say is done with a pure heart, a clear mind, and with words that speak in love. I pray Lord that I live worthy of Your glory, and that You will call me Your good and faithful servant.

Hebrews 4:13 NIV

~~~~~

"But you are a chosen people, a royal priesthood, a holy nation, God's special possession, that you may declare the praises of him who called you out of darkness into his wonderful light."

Thank You God for choosing me! Thank You for this reminder......I am somebody special, even if others think otherwise! So Lord, because You have given me life through Your Word, and have accepted me into Your marvelous light, I am forever grateful. I pray for continuous sight in the light, so that I can see Your purpose for me. Give me strength and endurance to walk in it graciously.

1 Peter 2:9 NIV

"Love does not delight in evil but rejoices with the truth. It always protects, always trusts, always hopes, always perseveres."

Thank You Lord God for showing me how to love; to love unconditionally and to love faithfully in spite of chaos and confusion provoked by others. Open my heart to love up close, and to be able to love from afar. To love during my storms, and to love when the sun shines. To love when I am weak and to love when I am strong. To love in truth and not in false hopes. To love in the light and not in darkness. Your Word also tells me that love is patient and kind, so Lord please show me how to execute these with others who are insensitive....show me how to love intentionally, deliberately and most of all unselfishly.

1 Corinthians 13:6-7 NIV

~~~~

"No one has ever seen God; but if we love one another, God lives in us and his love is made complete in us."

Your Word says to treat others as I would want to be treated, and so Lord open my heart to treat all people in love. Open my heart to those who have closed hearts and who treat others with malice and manipulation. Even those who treat me wrong, Lord open my heart and give me a response that mirrors Your Will and Your Way. Continue to show me how to love myself first so that I have the ability to love others just as much, and to love unconditionally. Thank You in advance Lord for filling my mind and my heart with feelings of love, so that my actions and reactions towards those things and others who don't know how to love is peaceful, joyful, and above all is respectful.

1 John 4:12 NIV

"For everyone who asks receives; the one who seeks finds; and to the one who knocks, the door will be opened."
Thank You Lord God for an open invitation to receive from You! I am humbled, grateful, and extremely thankful. I know I have to do my part: pray, fast and read Your Word, and so Lord provide me with strength daily to run this race we call life. When opportunities come, give me the confidence to open the doors to see new possibilities. Clear my mind of any fear, and give me wisdom to know what doors to open and what doors to keep closed. Direct my path Lord!
Matthew 7:8 NIV

~~~~~

"Whoever conceals their sins does not prosper, but the one who confesses and renounces them finds mercy."
Lord I confess and pray for forgiveness of sins that I have committed knowingly and unknowingly. Thank You for Your Love and Your Mercy! Thank You for the many opportunities to redo, rethink and recommit my ways, thoughts and actions so that I am aligned with Your Will and Your Way.
Proverbs 28:13 NIV

"pray continually, give thanks in all circumstances; for this is God's will for you in Christ Jesus."

Lord God Your Will is my Will. I will humbly follow Your Word and Your Way so that I can walk in Your marvelous light. Thank You for the strength to persevere through my long days to pray circles around those things and people who I am thankful for, and for those things that I desire like peace, joy and happiness. Thank You for clearing the white noise from my hearing so that I can clearly hear Your directions. Thank You for keeping my mind focused on good things so that stinking thinking does not consume my every thought. Thank You for a pure heart so that I can easily forgive those who offend me. Thank You Lord God for Your protection so that in the midst of my storms, I still feel blessed. Thank You for equipping me with faith as small as a mustard seed, so that I can patiently wait on You to fulfill Your promises. Thank You God for just being You!

1 Thessalonians 5:17-18 NIV

"Cast all your anxiety on him because he cares for you."

Thank You Lord for caring as much as You do, You take my pain away, You give me peace, I am so thankful that I know You. I sometimes have those moments when I am not sure what to do; I am reminded of Your Word that tells me to have faith in You. I thank You for wrapping Your arms around me and squeezing me tight, thank You for keeping me in Your marvelous light. Lord I pray for family and friends too, I pray that they find peace in the midst of their storms because they know how to bring their burdens to You.

1 Peter 5:7 NIV

"For every house is built by someone, but God is the builder of everything."

Thank You God, for I know my life is still under construction. Thanks be to You, I am stronger, wiser and more confident. My strength comes from fasting, reading Your Word, and praying continuously. I trust and have faith in Your promises. Because of the foundation in love You layed, I can stand tall during adversity, I can rejoice in sadness, and I can be hopeful in hopeless situations. Thank You for Your meticulous handiwork.

Hebrews 3:4 NIV

~~~~~

"There is surely a future hope for you, and your hope will not be cut off."

Thank You Lord God for Your promise to provide me a future that will be prosperous and full of hope. Continue to order my steps so that I walk in the way that is pleasing to You. Give me strength to move any barriers that may exist, so that my walk is clear of those things and people who cause adversity. Open my eyes wide so that I can see clearly. Get rid of the white noise so I can hear clearly, and organize my thoughts so I speak clearly. Thank You in advance for these blessings, and the hope for many more.

Proverbs 23:18 NIV

> "I am the vine; you are the branches. If you remain in me and I in you, you will bear much fruit; apart from me you can do nothing."

Thank you Lord! I have no intentions to disconnect myself from You! I am so grateful that You find me worthy enough to remain connected to me. Thank You for providing me the strength to hang on this long absorbing Your Word into me. Because of my steadfast diet, I am much stronger and wiser. I know that I am nothing without You. With You I am everything; at peace, full of joy, and I feel whole! Thank You for the connection.

John 15:5 NIV

Strength In the Lord

> "And as for you, brothers and sisters, never tire of doing what is good."

Thank You Lord for this reminder in Your Word. ...never give up, even when I don't see the light at the end of the tunnel.....keep pushing. There are times when I want to stop addressing issues that belong to me, and those that belong to other people, because it becomes exhausting. Especially when the response is stagnant. So Lord, help me to see Your light when complacency sets in. Help me to remember that my strength comes from You, and all I have to do is ask for help. When I become weak, make me strong in my mind and in my heart. Give me the courage to use my voice when my passion does not align with the bureaucratic way. Give me hope, and remind me that my work is Your work, and that my actions and reactions are not done in vain.

2 Thessalonians 3:13 NIV

"Get rid of all bitterness, rage and anger, brawling and slander, along with every form of malice."
Oh Lord I pray that if I experience negative encounters with others, that I do not hold grudges, or develop any animosity against them. I pray that even if I have been offended, that my heart remains pure and filled with joy, love and peace.
Ephesians 4:31 NIV

~~~~

"Consider him who endured such opposition from sinners, so that you will not grow weary and lose heart."
Oh Lord Jesus I will not complain! Forgive me for wanting more than I deserve, and for desiring what I was not supposed to have. I am grateful for what You have allowed me to have....my family, friends, home, job, finances, and all of the other extra blessings! Please forgive me Lord for those times that I complained; not satisfied with the challenges that I sometimes encountered. Continue to show me how to endure in the midst of adversity, and still respond with a heart full of love, peace and joy.
Hebrews 12:3 NIV

"Follow God's example, therefore, as dearly loved children and walk in the way of love, just as Christ loved us and gave himself up for us as a fragrant offering and sacrifice to God."

Thank You Lord God for this reminder in Your Word....to show love in all that I do and say; with all people at all times. Honestly praying Lord, sometimes this is difficult! So when I find myself in situations where others are involved, and those moments are unpleasant, please give me the words, and the appropriate tone and body language that communicate a response in love. I pray that even when I get angry, disappointed, betrayed, and mistreated, that my response is in love.

Ephesians 5:1-2 NIV

~~~~~

"No one should seek their own good, but the good of others."

Thank You Lord for this reminder in Your Word that teaches me that it is better to give then to receive. Continue to purify my heart with thanksgiving; suspending my self-interest so that I can serve those who are in need. Thank you for minimizing prideful thinking and strengthening my desire to help others without judgment. Continue Lord to use me and the gifts that You have blessed me with for Your glory and for all people.

1 Corinthians 10:24 NIV

"This is how we know what love is: Jesus Christ laid down his life for us. And we ought to lay down our lives for our brothers and sisters."
Thank You Lord for this clarification in Your Word. I do appreciate Jesus's sacrifice. And so Lord, whatever You would have me to do, for whomever You would have me to do it for, provide me the ability to do it! Show me my gifts so that they can be used for Your glory. Give me the wisdom and the discernment to know what people need, and let my actions be ministered in love.
1 John 3:16 NIV

~~~~~

"Let us hold unswervingly to the hope we profess, for he who promised is faithful."
Oh Lord thank You for Your promises! When I think of Your goodness, and all that You have done for me, my soul cries out.....Thank You Lord for loving me! Help me to keep my mind free of doubt and my thoughts absent from fear, I am praying always for Your presence to be near. Help me to stand strong on solid ground, in You joy, peace, and love I have found. I pray for truth in all that I say and do, Lord keep my heart transparent when it comes to loving and honoring You.
Hebrews 10:23 NIV

"Nothing in all creation is hidden from God's sight. Everything is uncovered and laid bare before the eyes of him to whom we must give account."
Oh Lord, I pray that everything I do and say are pleasing in Your sight. I pray that my daily interactions with others are committed in joy, peace, and thanksgiving. I pray for a disappearance of all known and unknown weaknesses that cause me to sin against You! Purify my heart with forgiveness for those situations from the past, and those that exist today, so that my heart is free of pain and anger, and opened up to give and receive love even when I have been offended. I know that what is done in the dark will eventually been seen in the light, so I pray that You guide my daily walk in and through the light. And when that day comes to join You in the home above, I pray that I am welcomed as Your good and faithful servant.
Hebrews 4:13 NIV

~~~~~

"Let your conversation be always full of grace, seasoned with salt, so that you may know how to answer everyone."
Let the words of my mouth and the meditation of my heart be acceptable in thy sight! I pray for sweet words when I speak, especially in the midst of frustration, disappointment, and anger. Give me a voice that speaks with wisdom and transparency. Lord seal my lips from speaking lies. I pray for a voice that speaks in truth, with integrity, at all times with all types of people.
Colossians 4:6 NIV

"Therefore, as God's chosen people, holy and dearly loved, clothe yourselves with compassion, kindness, humility, gentleness and patience."

Thank You Lord! Daily I do my best to display these characteristics towards all people. Please convict my spirit when You see that I have reacted differently, especially with those people who do not carry themselves in this manner. Sometimes, it is easier to respond in the same evil behavior as them, especially if I have been offended. Keep me from taking offense to their weakness! I am reminded in Your Word that vengeance is Yours, and You will protect me from evil! Two wrongs do not make it right! Thank you! I pray for an abundance of patience to be able to express my gentleness with others who are still immature in their thinking and in their actions as adults. Create in me a clean heart to be able to respond in love even when that feeling has not been reciprocated by others. Give me peace in my mind, and in my heart to treat others as I would want to be treated.....even when they are not nice.

Colossians 3:12 NIV

God's Presence, Peace and Protection

"My dear brothers and sisters, take note of this: Everyone should be quick to listen, slow to speak and slow to become angry, because human anger does not produce the righteousness that God desires."
Thank You God for this reminder in Your Word. ..observe, listen and think before I spew evil. Honestly, this is sometimes difficult to do, especially when my emotions are involved. I pray Lord that You will hold my tongue when my thoughts are fixed on negative thinking. Give me the wisdom to know when it just isn't worth my time, integrity and most importantly, my promised blessings....help me to close my mouth! Let the words of my mouth and the meditation of my heart be acceptable to Your sight.
James 1:19-20 NIV

~~~~~

"God is just: He will pay back trouble to those who trouble you"
Thank You God for Your promise to provide protection from others who offend me, mistreat me, and for those who take me for granted. You are a just God and I have to remind myself of Your Word. ....vengeance is Yours! I know that I can make a mess of things when I try to do things my own way. So give me strength to stand still and let You fight my battles. Provide me the patience to wait on You so You can get the glory. Please, please shut my mouth from speaking the negative thoughts in my mind. Instead give me the words to speak of Your goodness and Your favor. Thank in advance for Your presence, guidance and Your love.
2 Thessalonians 1:6 NIV

"Let your conversation be always full of grace, seasoned with salt, so that you may know how to answer everyone."
Let the words of my mouth and the meditation of my heart be acceptable in thy sight! I pray for sweet words when I speak, especially in the midst of frustration, disappointment, and anger. Give me a voice that speaks with wisdom and transparency. Lord seal my lips from speaking lies. I pray for a voice that speaks in truth, with integrity, at all times with all types of people.
Colossians 4:6 NIV

"Whoever of you loves life and desires to see many good days, keep your tongue from evil and your lips from telling lies."
Lord I pray that I live a life that sees a lot of good days. My daily prayer is to use my mouth in a manner that gives You the glory every time I open my mouth. Even when I am upset, I pray with intention to still speak words of peace....I really need help with this Lord! Give me strength to hold any negative thoughts, show me how to make the best out of every situation, and look to You for direction.
Psalm 34:12-13 NIV

Daily Spiritual Nugget

"For those who exalt themselves will be humbled, and those who humble themselves will be exalted."
Thank You Lord Jesus for this reminder. ...I am nothing without You, with You I am blessed! Everything that I have, and all that I am able to do, Lord I give You the honor and the glory. I pray daily for Your presence, wisdom, Your direction, and I am careful to follow Your Will and Your Way. Every now and then I admit that I stray on my own path - thank You Lord Jesus for Your protection and love that guides my feet back on solid ground. With You I am safe! You are my shelter in the storm. You protect me from those who try to harm me, and You provide comfort when I am feeling uncomfortable during life's challenges. And because of all of Your attention on me, I am forever grateful and humble myself before You!
Matthew 23:12 NIV

~~~~~

"Be very careful, then, how you live—not as unwise but as wise, making the most of every opportunity, because the days are evil."
Lord I pray that You will provide me with the type of wisdom that will guide me, protect me, and allow me to discern what is good and in my best interest. As one door closes and another opens, Lord put my feet on the right path. Give me the sight to see the possible bumps in the road, and provide me the strength to go around, or the courage to go through. I pray that every encounter I have with a blessing or with an obstacle, that I don't forget to give You the glory, the honor and the praise.
Ephesians 5:15-16 NIV

"Everyone who calls on the name of the Lord will be saved."

Thank You Lord God for making it so easy......I just call out Your name and I am protected. Your name, one above all others is a name that loves unconditionally, forgives faithfully, and blesses abundantly. Oh how I love Your name! Give me the wisdom to know when to call on You in need and not in vain. I pray that the power in Your name continues to fall upon me; delivering me from those things that keep me bound in fear, negativity and depression. I will praise Your name every chance I get. Oh Lord Your name will be a name I never forget.

Romans 10:13 NIV

"Let everything that has breath praise the Lord. Praise the Lord."

Lord I praise Your Holy name with all that I have. I praise You with my mouth, I am so blessed to have You guide me down a righteous path. I praise You with my mind with every thought I try my best to honor You, I am so thankful for You turn my rainy days into skies of blue. I praise You with my heart for it will always belong to You, I am grateful for Your promise to do all that You say You will do. Lord I praise You through my storms because I trust You wholeheartedly, I love You because You protect me from the enemy.

Psalm 150:6 NIV

"For the word of the Lord is right and true; he is faithful in all he does."
Lord God thank You for Your Word! I use Your Word as a blueprint to direct my daily walk in this sometimes chaotic place we call life. Your Word provides me clarity on how to be alive and live blessed and have abundantly in this world, and at the same time to be dead to the false gods in this world. Your Word provides me a understanding of what unconditionally love feels, look and acts like. Your Word teaches me how to love those who offend me. It shows me how to live in peace with a storm raging all around me. Yes Your Word is just right for my mind, body and soul. It gives me the tools to fight life's battle with courage, charisma, and in good character. Your Word is alright by itself and by itself heals the heartbroken, gives strength to the weak, and hope to the hopeless. Thank You for Your everlasting Word!
Psalm 33:4 NIV

"If we confess our sins, he is faithful and just and will forgive us our sins and purify us from all unrighteousness."
Oh Lord I am far from perfect, and so daily; minute by minute, hour after hour I pray for forgiveness for any thoughts, actions and reactions committed knowingly and unknowingly that do not align with Your Will and Your Way. Thank You Lord for helping me to keep my heart pure, free from evil, and my lips from telling lies. I pray for strength for those times when I am confronted with evil; chaos and confusion, dysfunction and disobedience. Lord protect my mind, body and soul!
1 John 1:9 NIV

"In the same way, faith by itself, if it is not accompanied by action, is dead."

Lord I thank you for Your continuous love and Your protection which allows me to stand strong in Your Word, and to stay faithful to Your Will and Your Way. Lord I trust in Your promises, and so I will do my part by praying, fasting, meditating, and reading Your Word daily. Thank You for providing me with clarity and instructions on how to apply it daily with every person and situation I engage. I pray that my actions reflect Your teachings and show myself approved. Thank You Lord for abiding in me!

James 2:17 NIV

"For it is with your heart that you believe and are justified, and it is with your mouth that you profess your faith and are saved."

Thank You Lord for showing me through Your Word, how to cleanse my heart so that it is free from animosity, anger, deceit and bitterness. With a purified heart I am able to love unconditionally, forgive without holding grudges, and have peace in the midst of chaos around me. Thank You Lord for providing hope in Your Word which allows me to believe in all that You promise to do! Thanks to You I am confident, and courageous. I believe and have faith in all that You do. I speak of Your goodness and Your love to all who will listen. Your name is above all other names, and so I call on You; Father, Son and the Holy Ghost to provide protection, direction, and salvation.

Romans 10:10 NIV

"Our God is a God who saves; from the Sovereign Lord comes escape from death."

Thank You God for Your promise to provide protection against the evil things in this world. I know I have to do my part by following Your precepts, and aligning my ways with Your Word. Daily I seek Your face in prayer, asking for Your forgiveness of any sinful acts; known and unknown, so that I may exist in Your marvelous light. Save me oh Lord!

Psalm 68:20 NIV

"May the God of hope fill you with all joy and peace as you trust in him, so that you may overflow with hope by the power of the Holy Spirit."

Oh Lord, I pray daily to be filled with Your Spirit. Help me to consume my thoughts with peace and joy. Even when chaos arises in my life; at work, at home, and with family and friends, I pray that Your Spirit speaks through me so that my actions and reactions are aligned with Your Will and Your Way. I trust in Your promises, and I stand in expectation with hope for a pure heart and a renewed mind.

Romans 15:13 NIV

"You are my refuge and my shield; I have put my hope in your word."
Oh God, You are my refuge, shield, deliverer, comforter; You are my all in all. I put my hope and trust in You for all the days of my life. When man lets me down, I know that You are always there to pick me back up. Thank You for Your love and protection against the evil in this world. Thank You for Your guidance through troubled times and chaotic moments. Thank You for delivering me from my wretched self, others, and from those things that kept me out of Your Will. Your Word feeds my heart and mind with praise, thanksgiving, peace and joy. Because of Your love I feel whole
Psalm119:114 NIV

~~~~~

"In him and through faith in him we may approach God with freedom and confidence."
Thank You Lord Jesus for bearing my burdens so that I may reverence the Father with a faith that is beyond measure. Because of Your suffering, I can walk upright without shame of wrongdoing. Thank You for providing me with the confidence to come to the Father with hope, and expectancy to receive an infinity of blessings. Because of You, I am stronger and wiser. I rejoice in the midst of uncertainty, because I trust with an open heart filled with love and thanksgiving. Thank You Father God for allowing me to be in Your presence.
Ephesians 3:12 NIV

"But the Lord is faithful, and he will strengthen you and protect you from the evil one."

Thank You Lord for Your protection from those who are not like You. I am so glad that I can call on You in times of distress, weakness, and sadness, to provide me just what I need to make it through. I know that it does not matter how big or small the issue is, You have my back! Thank You for Your strength which allows me to stand tall and stand still, patiently waiting for You to see me through some of life's issues.

2 Thessalonians 3:3 NIV

"The Lord is a refuge for the oppressed, a stronghold in times of trouble."

Thank You Lord for Your availability during those moments when life seems unbearable. Thank You for the strength that keeps me from engaging in addictive behaviors to try and take my pain away. I am so thankful that You do not mind bearing my burdens and instead You take them and make all things new. Your presence brings me hope that a better day is coming on the horizon. In Your Word I find strength, peace and joy. Thank You for providing me the coverage to take new risks and trusting You to do what You promised to do. I pray that family, friends and even my enemies in times of need, find joy in the morning because they know and depend on You to get the help that they need.

Psalm 9:9 NIV

"Love the Lord your God with all your heart and with all your soul and with all your strength."
Lord God I love You, honor You, and will worship You forever with everything I am, and all that I have. My strength is because of You, and all that You promise to do. My heart is wide open to give and to receive. Because of You I can breathe. Thank You for my existence. Because of You I have peace, thank You for helping me to think clearly. Because of You I have courage; I can walk with my head up high and not in shame. It is because of You that I rejoice when others try to steal my joy.
Deuteronomy 6:5 NIV

~~~~~

"Blessed is the one you discipline, Lord , the one you teach from your law; you grant them relief from days of trouble, till a pit is dug for the wicked."
Thank You Lord for the teaching of Your Word. It provides me with instructions on who to fellowship with, what to eat and wear, and how to seek You so that I live free from the bondage of sin, reaping a continuous flow of blessings. Your Word says that You chastise those You love, so Lord I don't mind Your correction. I know I may question Your motives at times for some of the challenges I face in my life, but I realize that You are just checking to see how much I depend on and how much I really trust You. I am careful to not take any credit for what I say I do, but to give You glory for all that You do! Thank You Lord God for Your Word that protects me from the evil ways of others gives me joy when I am sad, and tells me how much You love me unconditionally.
Psalm 94:12-13 NIV

"For it is not the one who commends himself who is approved, but the one whom the Lord commends."
Oh Lord continue to show me how to be in Your perfect Will. Please forgive me of any self-righteous talk or ways that may deny You from getting the glory. I pray that You see me worthy enough to keep Your light shining through me, so that it is You Lord that gets the glory and honor. I pray for a humbled Spirit, absent of selfishness, and self-serving ideology.
2 Corinthians 10:18 NIV

~~~~

"And the peace of God, which transcends all understanding, will guard your hearts and your minds in Christ Jesus."
Thank you God for Your everlasting peace; peace in my heart, and peace in my mind. At times it is difficult to avoid the feelings that often come from being angry, frustrated, disappointed, anxious, and impatient. My carnal thinking wants to kill, destroy and retaliate. But thanks be to You the God that loves me unconditionally! When chaos arises, You send the Holy Spirit to comfort me. Your Word reminds me of Your greatest sacrifice, and the peace upon Your Son when He died up on the cross to pay the price for our sins. How dare I not be at peace! God I pray that family and friends find the peace that they may be searching for. I pray that for some, in spite of the realities of health issues, inadequate finances, job related stresses, and failed relationships & friendships, Your PEACE must be sought and achieved!
Philippians 4:7 NIV

"This is what the Lord says: "Restrain your voice from weeping and your eyes from tears, for your work will be rewarded," declares the Lord........"
Thank You Lord! Your Word also tells me to endure; joy does come in the morning. Give me strength to endure. So I will wait for my victory. I will wait for my deliverance. I will wait on Your perfect timing. It is comforting to know that my tears are not in vain. Thank You Lord for all of Your blessings.
Jeremiah 31:16 NIV

~~~~~

"A gentle answer turns away wrath, but a harsh word stirs up anger."
Lord God I pray that the words that come out of my mouth are filled with love, compassion, and respect. That even in the midst of frustration and chaos, my words will still be pleasing to Your hearing. When others use words to hurt, harm and manipulate, Father God help me to refrain from responding in a manner that does not give You the glory. Give me the courage to stand tall and be at peace, knowing that You will take care of those type of people in Your time. Shine Your light on me, so that others will see You in me. Let Your Will be done! Hallelujah!
Proverbs 15:1 NIV

"But you are a chosen people, a royal priesthood, a holy nation, God's special possession, that you may declare the praises of him who called you out of darkness into his wonderful light."

Thank You God for choosing me to walk in Your marvelous light. I honor and adore You for teaching me how to live right. Your Word teaches me how to get back up when the evil of this world tries to knock me down, comfort, peace and joy, in Your Word I have found. Through sickness, chaos, and trials & tribulations, because of Your light, Your Word has revealed holy revelations. I praise You and honor You because Your Word continuously renews my thinking, when life presents me with challenges, it is Your Word that keeps me from stinking thinking. Thank You Holy Spirit for reminding me to walk in faith with kingdom principles, I put all my trust in You, because with You all things are possible. Thank You for the strength to pray circles around my dreams and hopes for the future, No weapon formed against me shall prosper!

1Peter2:9 NIV

"Surely God is my salvation; I will trust and not be afraid. The Lord, the Lord himself, is my strength and my defense; he has become my salvation."

Thank You Lord God for just being You! Time after time Your presence carries me through. Through my storms, trials and tribulations, through Your Word I have found so many peaceful revelations. Unlike man, I trust You with my heart and mind, in times of chaos and confusion Your joy in the morning comes right on time. Thank You for delivering me from those things that cause me to fall; thank You for Your son's sacrifice at the cross he paid it all. I know I am still a work in progress and You're not done with me yet, I will pray continuously for Your protection and direction and for my mind to be kept. Please Lord continue to purify my heart and renew my thinking daily. Even in times of anger and frustration, I pray my words have a peaceful delivery. Oh Lord I trust You with all that I am, thank You for being my very best friend!

Isaiah 12:2 NIV

Thank you Lord for all of your blessings. Thank you Lord for guiding me in the right direction. Thank you for allowing me to live one day at a time, thank you Lord for your presence right on time. Thank you for your light that guides my walk each and every day, thank you for the strength to kneel every morning and pray. Thank you for visions of things yet to come, thank you for waking me every morning in my right mind and with wisdom. Thank you for the peace you give in the midst of the chaos, thank you for the joy that comes in the morning and giving me hope that my life is not lost. Thank you for your grace and mercy, thank you for teaching and showing me in your word how to live holy.

Daily Spiritual Nugget